MW01170524

On America

On America

Art Callaham

On America

© 2021 Arnold Callaham

Published in the United States of America by
High Peaks Publishing
www.highpeakspublishing.com

Cover design and production by Silverback Designs
Editorial services by High Peaks Publishing

ISBN: 978-1-7377313-3-7

This book is dedicated to Mrs. Ruth Anne Cardwell Callaham, my wife, and my best friend forever, who for over 50 years, through good times and bad times, has made me the person I am today. The vote is still out if that person is good or bad, yet, know this—that person is happy to have found her, married her and loved her for all times.

Table of Contents

Introduction

Who are the "Americans"? Well, I believe you are one of them. Why? Because you bought this book and at least are reading the introduction.

Enough questioning, you didn't buy this book to take a test. So let me tell you who I believe the Americans are. Many are Democrats and others are Republicans—I for one am a Republican. Some are conservatives, while others plead that they are liberals—in reality most, including me, are moderates—in the middle.

Some Americans believe in abortion, but not in abortion as murder or as a convenient method of birth control—that's really a middle-of-the-road position. Same with the death penalty: Some believe in its use as a deterrent for crime, but those same believers would never use the death penalty to kill those who are mentally disturbed or as a deterrent for innocent people convicted of a crime.

Yes, middle of the road. You or me, either one of us, could go on and on about national defense, foreign aid, affirmative action and any one of a vast number of social and political issues that frame conservative vs. liberal arguments. Few, if any of us, would take an absolute stand, spear-in-the-ground, on any issue.

A good friend of mine, Tim Rowland, a newspaper columnist for a regional newspaper, wrote a column several years ago where he postulated that eighty percent of all Americans were in the "center" with ten percent each on the left and right fringe.

Sadly, as Tim went on, it is the fringe, either left or right, who are the loudest, say the most and work the hardest to convince or convert those of us in the middle to a particular fringe point of view. More so, it's comfortable in the middle, and most of us are willing to let the ten percent, and sometimes a lesser percentage, rule the day on issues that are truly important to us. This is a sad truth about many of us who are Americans.

My hope is that, after reading this book, you will become more vocal about your centrist convictions. That vocalness is what will make you an American. Our forefathers, if nothing else, were vocal about their beliefs; most were willing to stand up for those beliefs. Americans today need to speak out about their personal convictions, so as not to let the vocal minority rule. Americans still believe in the concept of the majority ruling.

Americans are old and young. Some are black, many are white and others fall into racial categories usually referred to by skin color—red, brown, yellow. But true Americans never refer to themselves as "Black-Americans" or "African-Americans" or "White-Americans" or "Japanese-Americans;" but rather call themselves simply "Americans." That's enough; being an American speaks for itself—either good or bad. Being an American is enough reward or enough condemnation in and of itself.

Americans are rich and poor and all those financial conditions in between. Wealth doesn't make a person "more American" and certainly a lack of wealth or even being poor doesn't close every door to advancement. Being an American speaks to hope and possibility. Americans do not need a politician to promise them either.

Americans do not want the color of their skin or the size of their bank account or their age, or their political beliefs to influence their success. Oh, many people are still looking for that edge, that shortcut to make success easier, the burden lighter, the race won—but those are not Americans, not by my accounting.

This book is divided into several sections: Family, Friends, War and Peace and finally this Country. Each section is made up of chapters that contain stories or opinion pieces. Some of the pieces are dated to add a contextual perspective. The opinion pieces are mine and the stories are generally factual, yet the names of folks in the stories are sometimes made up. Some of the stories are written in the first person with the "I" assumed to be me—wrong. Some of the "I" stories are about me; however, many are compilations of stories I've heard from others.

I'm no hero, I'm not a great athlete and I certainly am not an absolutely wonderful person. At the very best I'm a story teller and an opinion writer. There are many warts on my pickle, some I'm not very proud of. There are a couple of stories that may sound risqué (and they probably are), but those stories speak to Americana. Not everyone is an "Ozzie" or a "Harriet" (you'll show your age if you remember the TV show). Some may object to the language in some of the stories, yet many Americans talk that way.

You will probably disagree with some, or all of the opinion-based chapters, however, some will agree with some and all will probably agree with some. Confused? Well, that is what opinions are all about. Above everything else I hope you enjoy the book. So, sit back and enjoy one man's view of Americans.

Section 1

FAMILY

The only rock I know that stays steady, the only institution I know that works, is the family.
—Lee Iacocca

Think of your family today and every day thereafter, don't let the busy world of today keep you from showing how much you love and appreciate your family.
—Josiah

Everyone has one, just like noses, or some would say assholes. Everyone has a family; sometimes the members of a family are unknown, or at the least not admitted to. But generally, we all have a recognizable family unit. Sometimes a family may include those not connected by blood or marriage or court order; these family members may include friends either physically present or imagined. Sometimes the gang or the team or even perceived enemies act as a member(s) of the family unit.

It is the family that oftentimes makes a person, and this section outlines a couple of family members who have had an impact on who I am today. My wife, parents, brother, in-laws and an uncle are mentioned in this section. Also, there are outsiders: coaches, girlfriend, teammates that for a period of time are like family and have had a role in molding me into the American I am today.

This section of the book is not all inclusive. I for one have a large family and yes, some of my family members are friends. I have, however, reserved another section of this book for more on friends.

This section also tells a bit about me personally, my likes and those things I don't like. Also, there is a Christmas wish list that transcends any specific time period. I believe any American can fit themselves into these chapters and imagine their own lives and the lives of their family. So, enjoy FAMILY.

Chapter 1
Stuff You Should Know

SYSK—your name
Taken from the podcast "Stuff You Should Know"

"Name him Arthur Arnold Callaham, Mac, we don't want a junior." my mom said to Doctor Buford McNeer from her bed at home. She had just given birth to her third child, second son, in October of 1948.

Blanche Carden Callaham, 44 years old in August of that year, thought she had a tumor when she went to see the doctor in June. She'd missed her period, had the hot flashes usually reserved for menopause, and then in early June a strange growth had pushed her belly out. Well, her dad had died early in life from cancer and Blanche thought her fate was sealed. "It must be a tumor," she told Arnold A. "Kelly" Callaham, her husband, before she went to see the doctor.

With a chuckle and a smile, the doctor, announced "Blanche, you won't believe this, but you're pregnant, about five months I'd say." With those reassuring words mom notified the local school board that she'd not be able to start back teaching in the coming school year. In those days a pregnant teacher, after the fifth month, could not be seen in the classroom by the children.

Heavens, they might figure out what "old so and so" was doing at night with her husband, or in the case of another high school teacher, with her latest boyfriend. And I guess teachers weren't 'sposed to be fornicating, copulating or "fuckin." Teachers were held to a higher standard in those days, kinda like the Catholic priests and nuns. Most everyone knew what they were really doing, but you didn't want the kids to know.

But hey, I didn't figure out what caused babies until I was 10 or 11—or was it the summer I met the strawberry blonde from Peterstown, at church camp, who took me out behind the girls' dorm and taught me how to kiss? Then showed me "first hand," if you will, the difference between boys and girls, and how some parts fit nicely together.

But here it was the new house on Tunnel Hill, recently built on the only land that mom's father had retained when he went bankrupt in the late '30s. Mom was an only child and when Granddad Carden died, the estate, not much more than the land, passed to Grandma Nell, who gave the land to mom and dad, sort of in return for them building a house and letting her live with them until she went to be with granddad.

Dad, "Kelly," was a railroader and mom was a teacher, and together they made an okay living and supported Grandma Nell and two kids, Caroline, the oldest, and until that evening in October, Bert the youngest.

I always thought Mom and Dad were great namers—namers of their children. Caroline, my sister, was Caroline Carden Callaham (CCC); Bert was Herbert Bertrum Callaham, Bert Bertram if you will, or BBC. And now I was Arthur Arnold Callaham, AAC. Most of our relatives referred to us as the "ABC" Callaham children. Cute, isn't it? As a youngster it just made me gag.

I guess I'd better clarify this early. Mom said to the doctor, who would ultimately record my birth at the courthouse—remember I was born at home—"name him Arthur Arnold." Well, aside from being one of the three doctors in our county, the doctor who delivered me was also a drinker.

So, after the home delivery (sounds like the post office came) the doctor crossed the road to my uncle's truck stop and tied one on, as the saying went in those days. A bit hung over the next day, the good doctor registered the birth of a male child born on October 19, 1948, at approximately 7:20 p.m.; mother, Blanche Carden Callaham; father, Arnold A. Callaham; name of the child "Arnold Arthur Callaham." Oops.

Nell Davis, the clerk of the Summers County Court, dutifully recorded the live birth in the permanent court record. See, I was a birth and I really wasn't a tumor. The error was not noticed until nineteen years later. In a close-knit community—Summers County had less than 20,000 residents and the town of Hinton less than 5,000—you could just call the clerk's office tell Nell that you wanted a copy of a birth certificate, give her the pertinent information, and she would hand write it, put the official seal on it and drop it in the mail. No one ever checked the permanent records, at least not for 19 years in my case.

Mom was a teacher, who went to school with Nell Davis, and had one of Nell's children in her class—why wouldn't Blanche Callaham know the particulars of her son's birth? So, in school, Little League, church, high school athletics, DeMolay, Key Club, college applications, summer camp registration and so on, all needing a birth certificate, mom would call, Nell would write, seal and mail. All was right with the world and young Arthur Arnold Callaham would be incorrectly registered because his real name was Arnold Arthur Callaham.

It ultimately took the United States Army to finally figure out who I really was (am). So, even if it takes 19 years to find out, your name is "stuff you should know."

Chapter 2
I Ain't too Keen On

*I try to stay away from negative stuff, but solely for the sake of
balance I present … things I ain't too keen on.*

—Julia Marchese

I have had folks tell me that they enjoyed or liked my writing,
and others have taken issue with me or have said in no short
terms that they didn't like what I had to say. Such is the way life
goes when you put your opinions and statements up for public
scrutiny. Really, I don't mind either those who like and/or those
who dislike what I have to say. It is the discourse that is important
in coming to a resolution about issues.

Mostly I write about what "I like"—really, I don't make up
stories to garner favor or agreement, nor do I write to generally
cause readers to dislike me or my writing. I like to write about
Americans, good or bad. So, I thought it might be interesting to
write about what "I don't like." Here goes!

I don't like unsigned or anonymous articles or statements that are
made public. Yes, I understand the concept: It gives voice to those
who might not otherwise avail themselves of the right to express
their feelings out of some sense of fear or trepidation concerning
signing or giving their name. But I have always felt that if you want
to say or write something you ought to be responsible enough to
sign or give your name.

I don't like all the fuss surrounding same-sex unions; to me this should be an argument about civil rights, not an argument about religious beliefs. From a religious perspective, I personally do not want to use the word "marriage" to describe a contract between a man and another man, or a woman and another woman. However, as there are civil rights that accrue to a man and a woman in a contract one with one another (which in the secular world we often refer to as "marriage"), therefore, I see no issue with affording those same civil rights to a man in contract with another man or woman with another woman.

We've got lots of lawyers and judges to sort out that contract language, so don't ask me to write the contract and don't ask me to amend my religious beliefs to sanction it. I believe God sanctions "marriage" between a man and a woman, and if you want that same sanction for other "unions," take it up with some spiritual consultant other than me. And oh, from my perspective, don't get the government, at any level to try to legislate my religious believes on this issue—that's between me and God. Civil rights are for everyone; spiritual and religious beliefs are between individuals and their individual perspectives about God.

I didn't like and certainly don't miss Osama bin Laden. Wish I had written this piece before his very timely departure from this world. The world does not know the total swath of human destruction contemplated, approved and in some cases executed by this subhuman, despotic creature. The world is a far better place without bin Laden in it. Now let's get rid of the copycat groups like ISIS, ISIL, DASH or whatever ruthless subhuman thugs like to refer to themselves as. God bless America.

One day a year I don't like Navy football. Yes, every year in early December when those "ruffians" from the Naval Academy beat up, as they have done for the past (too many) years, on my beloved Army Black Knights of the Hudson, I generally curse the ground on which they walk. However, due to the spectacular and heroic work of those Navy Seals—some of whom were part of the

Navy victories over Army—in ridding the world of bin Laden, let me just say "Go Navy!"

I don't like to see trousers worn below the waist that expose undergarments and/or more. To me that is classless. I don't like ball caps worn anyway other than with the bill forward. In fact, I don't like to see hats of any kind worn by men indoors. Those are norms my mom taught me, and I bet yours taught you the same things. To all of the mothers who taught their children, even when those children didn't listen, may God also bless you.

There you have it, some of the things I don't like—obviously, those who know me realize that this is only the short list—there are others. I will list some of them later, and I bet many Americans will agree with me.

Chapter 3
Golf

*No one will ever have golf under his thumb. No round ever
will be so good it could not have been better. Perhaps this
is why golf is the greatest of games. You are not playing a
human adversary; you are playing a game. Would that life
was the same!*

—Bobby Jones

Count up two checkoffs on my own personal bucket list. Several years ago, over a Father's Day weekend and the week preceding, I attended the U.S. Open golf championship and was "inside the ropes" on three separate days—that's one. And I also made the cover of Sports Illustrated (well, maybe by association), that's two. My checkoffs and the quote by Bobby Jones need a lot of explaining, so, here goes.

Three years before I went to the U.S. Open, a group from our Country Club volunteered at the AT&T National Golf Tournament. The AT&T tournament was played at Congressional Country Club in Bethesda, Maryland. A year later this volunteer work consisted of marshaling Hole Number 10 during the tournament. Marshaling work is considered "inside the ropes," since Marshals are in fact inside on the playing field, up close with the professional golfers and actually inside the golfers' work space.

At the AT&T Tournament there was a contest to determine which group of marshals did the best job during the tournament, and cash prizes were awarded. Our country club's marshals won $25,000 as the best group that year. The entire community benefited from this effort, as the cash was divided and given to several local not-for-profits.

Fast forward one more year, the AT&T tournament was moved to Philadelphia as preparations were being made at Congressional for the U.S. Open. The folks at Congressional called and asked our club if we would like to marshal a hole at the Open. It didn't take long to provide that answer—a resounding YES. Because of the number of volunteers required by the USGA, our crew was augmented with some local folks, as well as a team from a nearby Virginia golf and country club. Sixty-plus marshals were needed to cover the seven days of the tournament. Our assignment was, once again, Hole 10.

As fate and skill would have it, a young man from Northern Ireland, Rory McIlroy, ran away from the field and won that year's U.S. Open. His picture on the tee at Hole Number 10, Sunday, Father's Day, in front of 45,000 excited golf fans, who were being kept quiet by the erstwhile marshals from Maryland and Virginia, adorned the cover of that week's Sports Illustrated. For true, I personally was off on Sunday, but I checked off my bucket list item by calling my claim-to-fame "guilt by association."

With that lead-in, what is there about golf and life? Well first, what is golf? Mark Twain said "golf is a good walk spoiled"— but a walk is not a race. Why is the sport of golf is called golf? Some would retort that all of the other good "four letter words" were taken. Golf is frustrating at times, causing visceral and vocal responses, yet seldom ending in the physical abuse of property or other humans. Others believe golf is an acronym for "gentlemen only, ladies forbidden;" yet today men and women, minorities and majorities of all nations enjoy the game. In fact, from an

American's perspective, several of the recent "number ones" in the golfing world were foreigners, and one is a minority. Just like life, golf, it is a-changin'.

Golf has only thirty-four rules; the Bible lists only ten or two commandants (you pick Old or New Testament); the U.S. Constitution, including all twenty-seven amendments, is only 17 pages long. In many ways each set of rules is pretty simple. In golf the players police themselves and seldom does the policing cause a fuss or physical confrontation—most golfers know and abide by the rules. Forty-five thousand fans, mostly Americans, watched a foreigner win America's own National Open and left the grounds in an orderly fashion; no city was burned, no riots occurred, no protesters arrested—maybe hockey and some political events could take a lesson.

In retrospect, this vignette should be titled: why aren't golf and life the same? Life should be enjoyed at a walk and not always at frantic pace. Life should be equal for all with no exclusions for age, race, religion, sex or national origin. Life shouldn't end in the physical or mental abuse of others caused by personal frustration. Wouldn't it be nice if life had few rules and each of us policed ourselves?

Today I'm thankful for getting to check two items off my personal bucket list—the checks allowed to me because I love golf and life. Tomorrow when I play golf I'll think again about a simpler and kinder life. That's what Americans should do.

Chapter 4
Christmas Wish List

*The Supreme Court has ruled that they cannot
have a nativity scene in Washington, D.C.
This wasn't for any religious reasons.
They couldn't find three wise men and a virgin.*

—Jay Leno

Author's note: This piece was originally written in 2012 and much more divisiveness has occurred since that time.

Americans love the Christmas season, so each year I like to have a Christmas wish list. "All I want for Christmas is my two front teeth:" These are the words to Donald Gardner's novelty Christmas Song written in 1944 while Gardner was teaching music to a second-grade class in Smithtown, New York. I've sung those words myself, with the usual "lisp" while awaiting new teeth to fill a gap in my smile. Today, in spite of the fact that I'm still missing a couple of teeth, my Christmas wish list is a bit more complex.

I know that the Christmas holiday season is a season for giving; however, the child in us all more often than not remains hopeful that Christmas and the New Year will be a time when some of our wishes come true.

Every day I wish and pray for peace on earth and goodwill among all mankind. Prosperity for all to include a roof overhead, enough to eat and drink and continued good health will always be on my list. I am appropriately thankful for the peace and prosperity that most Americans have today and I continue to pray for those who don't have it. Beyond that thankfulness, here is my wish list.

Nationally, I wish for reason and sensibility to return to the Congress of the United States. Similar to the Know Nothing Party (their actual name was the American Party) of the 1850's, fringe groups as well as the traditional national parties have polarized their own members to the extent that significant necessary legislation cannot move forward.

The Know Nothings of their time were bent on eliminating immigration and their uncompromising approach fueled riots and demonstrations that looked a lot like the "occupy" movements. A reasonable and sensible Congress focused on the American people, not reelection; willing to compromise on issues, not principles, working across party lines, could return this nation to the greatness achieved over the past two hundred years. If this wish comes true, then Congress might once again "know something."

I wish for major tax reform, both nationally and within the states and localities. Settling on one word to describe the act of paying for government would be a great start. Tax, fee, and most recently surcharge all have the same core meaning. A friend of mine described "surcharge," the latest politically correct term for how we pay for government, in profiling terms: "Let's add a surcharge to the rich." Sounds like, "let's strip search people who are not like us."

Taxation should be fair and equitable (I could live with some degree of graduated tax) instead of the current "some pay all." Let's move to "all pay some." Regardless of your feelings about former presidential candidate Herman Cain—and let's not argue about the specific percentages—his "9-9-9" flat rate tax proposal made sense to me. On the state level, Pennsylvania has had a generally flat personal income tax rate and it seems to work.

In all states I wish for significant tort reform and major changes in the way monies from fenced "trust funds" are allocated. Also, in the health care arena all three legs of the proverbial health care stool (provider, insurer and the tort system) need makeovers, or health care costs will ultimately make affordable and available health care a thing of the past.

As for transportation funding, we can no longer allow mass transit to suck up the majority of transportation dollars while local roads continue to degrade. In both cases, tort reform and transportation funding, I don't have a solution. So, my wish is for someone who does to come forward.

On local levels, I'll continue to wish for co-locations or consolidations of governmental services like police, fire and rescue, plans and permits, zoning, telephone service, information technology services, personnel services, vehicle maintenance, and procurement services. Tradition and parochialism cost millions of dollars each year.

In today's technology driven era we have the capability to economically and efficiently provide services without the requirement for separate organizations, facilities and the inherent overhead such separation brings. Finally, I wish that all governments would simply implement more, and study less.

I know that I've been too political, so, my simple wish is for you to have a Merry Christmas and a Happy New Year. If that wish offends you for some religious or secular reason then lift out the words Christmas and New Year and wish for me, in your own way, a merry and happy time of the year, because that is what I truly wish for you.

Chapter 5
Fathers

*Being a role model is the most powerful form of
educating ... too often fathers neglect it because they get
so caught up in making a living,
they forget to make a life.*

——John Wooden

We celebrate "Father's Day" on a Sunday in June each year, and I'd like to share a few memories and impressions of my father that have stayed with me for many years.

Fathers are a "different breed of cat," or so Byron Nelson, the great golfer, might have said. Nelson actually referred to winners as the ultimate different breed of cat and that comparison, between winners and fathers, might well reflect how special fathers can be.

Or is that *should* be? We hold up winners, in all aspects of life, to be special, and obviously some fathers should also be considered winners. Some fathers stick around through thick and thin and help raise their children; however, some don't.

Some fathers create an atmosphere of love and caring around their child or children; some don't. To me, my father was somewhere in between. Yes, he stuck around, but an atmosphere of love and caring, at least in the years when I grew up, was not exactly apparent to me.

Now don't take any of this the wrong way. I loved my father, and cried when he passed away nine days before my mother; however, I'm not sure that I always liked him. Dad was strict, profane and very direct. To a thirteen-year-old (and that was the year when I was sure my Dad lost his mind, not to get his mind back until I was thirty years old) strict, profane and direct didn't sit well.

Needless to say, for almost twenty years my Dad and I didn't get along. For those twenty years I missed many of the things in life that young people like me should learn from their dads.

The following few paragraphs are from my brother, and illustrate what a rebellious young kid missed when that kid—me—thought he knew more than his dad.

From my brother Bert: "Some events are very clear in my mind, and defined me when I became a dad. It was my father who showed me what it meant to be of service to others and what it meant to be a dad.

"Our high school played sports in West Virginia's Coalfield Conference; in those days Hinton High School was a Double A school in size. We played against several of the larger Triple A schools each year in football, basketball and track."

"My senior year we played Oak Hill, Triple A, as an away game in late October. That year a very unusual Arctic cold front descended on southern West Virginia during the week of our game. When we arrived in Oak Hill, the temperature was in the low 20s and falling. After our warm-up exercises, we returned to the field house for a brief period of time prior to the start of the game, basically to just get warm.

"Dad worked on Fridays until 3 p.m. and generally would not make it to all of my away games. I had not seen dad while we were doing our warmups and I suspected he would not make it to the game. As our team went back onto the field, one of my buddies punched me on the arm and said, 'look at your dad on the sidelines.' Sure enough he was there, and he had somehow found and brought with him, two 25-gallon oil drums. He had a fire going in both; keep in mind that this happened 'back in the day' when no such thing as heated benches existed.

"I don't know where he found the wood to burn, but he kept those fires going for the entire game. This is just one example of my dad giving back and not asking anything in return. I gained a new respect for him that cold fall night and learned that helping others when they don't expect it makes you a better person."

I miss my dad today and wish I had respected him more than I did "back in the day" when I was growing up. My brother figured it out, and I didn't. It took me until my dad was gravely ill to recognize what my brother figured out years earlier.

So, for all the dads who read this, some advice: Stick around and raise your kids; that is your responsibility. Show concern for others, it might just rub off. And kids (from six to sixty), respect your dad and get to know him. He's probably a winner in spite of what you think.

Chapter 6
Redheads

*Once in his life every man is entitled to fall
madly in love with a gorgeous redhead.*
—Lucille Ball

I, on the other hand, took this entitlement twice, and the second time I have remained married and faithful for over fifty years. Ah, but the first time was a really interesting time. I'm really not very good at writing about sex, love or rock and roll. You see, my mom always told me to respect women, honor women and always remember my manners. Sure, I am not a prude, or gay, or unwilling to look at or touch those of the fairer sex; my wife still believes I'm a sex fiend—remember, that's why I married a redhead. I've had my share of lovers, but my first love and a few others mentioned in this book are all the stories that I'll recount.

I was 14 and she was 15; the place was church camp. The time was June 1963. I bet if he were alive today, Irby Creager (our pastor) still wouldn't believe all that went on at the church's youth retreat that year. Although memorable for many reasons that I'll recount here, I still can't remember her name, only that she was visiting one of my classmates and came from a nearby town (I won't mention the town's name for fear someone else may be able to recall exactly who I'm writing about—remember my mom's

35

warning: "respect women, honor women and always remember your manners— men never tell.")

She was a strawberry blond according to her verbal resume, but she looked like a redhead to me, had a few freckles, a nice bosom (that's what good girls called "nice tits") for a 15-year-old, long legs that went from the ground all the way up to … You get the picture. Me, I was average height, full curly brown hair, a little on the stout side and pretty naïve about a lot that year. You see, I'd never been "laid," but that was about to change.

The camp lasted six days, running from Monday afternoon until Sunday after a morning church service. The days were full of games, crafts and a smattering of religious classes—it was church camp. The evenings were set aside for devotionals, scripture lessons and lots of singing. Three "hots and a cot," boys in one cabin, girls in another, lights out a 10 p.m. and get up at 6 a.m.—pretty standard stuff, it was church camp.

It was around eleven at night when the real fun started. Our chaperones were fairly old and usually worn-out from herding teenagers all day. So, by 10:15 the chaperones were sound asleep and the slipping out of cabins began. Now most of the kids were asleep along with the adults, however there were a few, boys and girls, who had other adventures on their mind, and sleep could wait. I was one, my good friend another, and the redhead and her friend made a nice foursome for a little petting and romance.

My good friend was "dating" the girl the redhead was visiting so I got tapped by my friend to entertain the redhead while he and his girlfriend got it on in the woods behind the cabins. Tuesday night was just a get acquainted time for me and the redhead. We talked and whiled away the time until my friend and his girl finished a session of "kissy face and huggee body"—then the four of us headed back to the appropriate cabins at around 2 a.m.

Just before sneaking back into camp the redhead asked me if I was a virgin. I replied truthfully that I was. She retorted that she wasn't, giggled and crawled through the window back into her cabin.

Next night we met for what I thought would be a repeat performance of sitting and talking—boy was I surprised when she showed up in a skirt and a loose-fitting blouse. It wasn't long until we were doing a little kissy face of our own and that led to a little touching around that beautiful bosom. Finally, after an hour of fooling around she asked me if I'd "show her mine" if she "showed me hers." I was so naive that I didn't know what she meant until she lifted her skirt and wasn't wearing any panties.

She undid my fly and pulled my organ out and began to lovingly stroke it. All the while she took my hand and placed it on her sex and explained how to put a finger, and later two, in and massage her while she continued to stroke me. It wasn't long before we both climaxed. This little ritual—kissing, touching, stroking and climaxing continued each night until the last night of camp.

On that Saturday night she took my hands and placed them on her shoulders while she straddled me (we were actually sitting on a large log covered with a blanket she had brought with her) and with one hand moved me into her. She told me to lean back and enjoy myself while she moved up and down on my shaft. Just before I climaxed, she stood up and ensured that I didn't cum in her. "There, you're not a virgin anymore."

After the Sunday morning church service, she was picked up by her parents, went home and I never saw her again. My buddy's girlfriend reported that she and her parents moved away at the end of the summer and I totally lost track of the redhead—but not the memories.

Chapter 7
Pardons

Pardon, old fathers.
——William Butler Yeats

Americans learned a great lesson in presidential power when then-President Jimmy Carter pardoned all those folks who fled America during the Vietnam conflict.

I for one and many of my friends admired those folks (I'll not call them Americans) for their personal courage. Their courage of conviction led them to leave the wonderful place we call America and migrate to another country. Although over a beer or two, or when I am in a boisterous mood, I might utter insults about their heritage, or mothers or their sexual orientation—yet, in my heart I never questioned their courage. Those folks were as brave as those Americans who served, and even as brave as those who gave their lives in defense of America and American values. Essentially those folks felt that serving America (and many thought that, in this conflict, America was unjust) was not among their convictions.

Many of those who served and or died did so because their country, America, asked or in the case of military conscription (you know, the draft) ordered them. I pissed my pants, as I'm sure many other Americans did, the first time I had a shot fired at me in anger. I'm sure many of those who left America pissed their pants when they got their draft notice. This pants pissing is an act motivated by fear and fear is a trigger for action—flight or fight. Fight (or in this case, service to America) is one manifestation of fear, flight is the one other. Fleeing America, just like fighting for (service to) America is an action, and when caused by fear, these actions are essentially the same. In reality both are understandable actions

And so, my friends, those of you who fled America and those of you who fought, I salute you; however, for those of you who fled, you will never receive my pardon if you return. Rudyard Kipling summed up my feelings in his epic poem Tommy: "For it's Tommy this, an' Tommy that, an' Chuck 'im out, the brute! But it's 'Savior of 'is country' when the guns begin to shoot." The true "saviors of our county" are those who fought, and those who fled and are now not accepting a pardon to return. To avoid my disdain and the disdain of many Americans those who "chucked themselves out," they need to continue their understandable action/courage of conviction and stay out.

Chapter 8
Baseball

*Athletes are born winners, they're not born losers, and the
sooner you understand this, the faster you can take on a
winning attitude and become successful in life.*
—Charles R. Sledge Jr.

Growing up, athletics was a very important part of my life. I
always liked to compete. Oh, I didn't always win, in fact I lost
more times than I can count.

Little League Baseball was my first sporting endeavor. I was
a catcher—you know, the "backstop" wearing the "tools of
ignorance." Great defense, fair hitter; but, no "gun" that great
catchers need to throw the ball "on a string" to the bases. I never
had that skill.

I played for Creed's Pharmacy, one of eight teams in the local
league. Creeds was a very competitive team; in the four years I
played for them we won the league championship two times, and
finished second in the other two years. We were led by Coach
Burdett in the dugout and "Wiggles" Skidmore on the field.

Coach, known to his players as "Cannonball," drove an old '51
Chevy sedan, and you could hear him coming to the field from
a mile away as he laid on the horn to let us know he was on the
way. Coach was a railroader, and like my dad, got off work at 3
p.m. and would rush to the practice field to be there by 4. For a

player, being late was not an excuse, as Coach Burdett was never late.

Wiggles, real name Jerry, was a year older than me, but twenty years older when it came to talent and knowledge of the game. (Wiggles moved away when he was 13 and our local league lost a real talent—some reported that he was killed in the Vietnam War). Wiggles pitched, played shortstop, led the league in hitting, had a gun and generally was the best player on the field—except maybe when D.K. Porterfield was playing.

Right up there with Wiggles and D.K. was another player on our team (Creed's Cardinals, red and white uniforms and caps; eat your heart out Bob Gibson and Dizzy Dean)—"Fatty" (real name Donnie) Man. Fatty was ambidextrous and could pitch equally well with either hand. In fact, Fatty won several back-to-back games by pitching left-handed in one and right-handed in the next. Fatty's exploits caused a rule change in Little League nationwide; pitchers may only pitch six innings in any seven-day period regardless of the arm they use. The rule didn't come into existence until a year after our All-Star team won two games in the Eastern Regional, both by Fatty, over a weekend.

Those two wins set us up for a finals game the following weekend—Wiggles threw a one hitter, walked two; yet we lost 1-0 and missed our chance to go to Williamsport for the World Series. I wasn't on that team, as I was cut from the All-Stars in favor of "J.O." Thompson who had a gun—his dad was one of the All-Star coaches.

Seriously, J.O. was a better catcher, better hitter and realistically did have a better arm. I forgave the slight when I was a senior in high school and Jack Thompson was reported to the principal for massaging his own private parts during an assembly, hence the nickname "J.O.". (You figure it out.)

My last year in Little League ended with a loss in the State Tournament final. Wiggles was gone and D.K. was our stud and he threw a two hitter, but walked six and we lost 3-2. I got a couple of hits in the tournament and actually threw out two runners at second—not bad for not having a gun. Later years found me in Senior League, Pony League and eventually in a fast pitch softball league before I left for the U.S. Army. I loved and still love baseball and softball, but whatever talent I have was better suited for football.

There is another vignette in this book that speaks to football, yet I still get excited each February when pitchers and catchers report to spring training in the Majors. And each year my wife and I take time out to watch the Men's College World Series; we've attended the Women's Softball World Series a couple of times and look forward to it each and every year. Americans love baseball and all of its derivatives; never forget that it is always "Baseball, Hot Dogs, Apple Pie and Chevrolet."

Chapter 8
Football

Winning isn't everything … it's the only thing."
—Vince Lombardi

As much as I loved baseball and still love it today, I was a better talent playing football. And hey, what the hell, high school football was my home town's passion. Not soccer, this was the 1960s and some in my home town had never even heard of the game, and not baseball or basketball or wrestling or track and field, just "smash mouth" football—Woody Hayes style. You line up your eleven boys and we'll line up our eleven and let's see who's still standing at the end of four quarters of play.

Oh, we had some pass plays in our playbook, but those were only for desperate moments. Our bread and butter running plays were "right, dive right" or "right, slant right" or even our very tricky (my tongue is in my cheek) "right, pitch right." We played an unbalanced line, wing T formation with exact plays either to the right or the left. This was *mano y mano* football, nothing very tricky.

Coach Bill Garten believed that the only way to win was to be stronger and faster than our opponent. Our strong side tackles called the blocking assignments, usually "wham," or wedge blocking, or "down," or slant blocking. Generally, you picked your target and blocked allowing the running back a split or lane to run through. Even the quarterback was expected to block someone once he handed off or pitched the ball. You see, in Garten's scheme if one man had the ball and the other ten blocked someone, then there was only one man left who could make the tackle. Therefore, each and every offensive player was in a man-on-man situation. Pretty simple stuff.

Watching game film, and I have to hand it to Coach, as we were one of the few schools if not the only school in our conference who filmed each game, was simply a grading exercise. On each play you got an A if you blocked someone and that someone did not make the tackle on your team's ball carrier. Any other result: missed block, no block, or your blocked person made the tackle was an F. Ball carriers fared little better. If you scored you got an A; if one man tackled you without scoring you got an F, if more than one man tackled you, you got an F and the men who obviously missed blocks or didn't block got ass chewings.

Garten's philosophy was to score on every play. "Why do we spend time practicing a play if we don't intend to score," he would rant. On defense we were a contain team—if you could make the opponent run ten plays before scoring, then you were successful.

Simple again, because most high school teams could not run ten successive plays without making a mistake and that mistake was what we were looking for. Our defensive scheme was an "Oklahoma 5-3 slant tackle with monster." We'd place the monster back on the offense's strong side and rotate the three defensive backs to that side also. The weak side of our defense would loop to the outside to contain sweeps or off-tackle slants; the nose guard would "play the piano" and was responsible for anything in the middle. Based upon the opponent's tendencies, the linebackers would slant left or right into lanes created when the slant tackle caused two or more blockers to try to block him.

I'm sure this sounds complicated, however the scheme tended to let two or more defensive players come free on every play to make tackles. Overall, our offense and defense were very simple schemes—we ran the ball and tried to contain the opponent's run game. Seldom did a high school use more than one or two pass receivers on any given pass play, so our three defensive backs were usually adequate to cover in passing situations.

Truthfully, I never liked Coach Garten and he only liked me when we won. Not that I was the cause of any loss, but Garten always blamed his players and laid no responsibility upon himself. Others on the team shared my opinion about Coach; but many, including my brother who played for him a few years before my time, loved and respected him. *C'est la guerre*, and war was what Garten wanted us to declare each time we went on the playing or practice field. A lesson I learned early in my playing days was that you don't have to be loved to be a good leader. And make no mistake, Coach was a good leader. My high school produced winning teams.

I had reasonable skills, and probably could have played on Saturdays in a small or medium sized college, but I injured my left knee in junior high school football and that injury cost me an opportunity to play for Marshall University in the late '60s. As history proved, that same injury may have saved my life when the Marshall football team was killed in a fiery plane crash on November 14, 1970. Had I continued at Marshall (I flunked out my freshman year) 1970 could have been my senior year—who knows, fate has a way of interceding in life.

But back to high school. I have so many memories of games played. Benny Hogan was one of our guards and he was blind in his left eye. As we grew up, Benny would sometimes remove his glass eye and wash it in his mouth just to gross out his buddies. When we ran a play to the right requiring Benny to pull and lead the blocking, obviously he would lead with his right eye. But when we ran a weak-side play to the left, Benny would pull and lead with his left eye. Usually no problem.

Arthur Adkins was our other guard—two good eyes. During one game Buck Yates, our quarterback or "QB," called "right, pitch right." This play called for both guards to pull and lead the blocking on the right. During that series of plays we had run right, pitch right a couple of times with little or no yardage gained—good time for a weak-side play like "right, pitch left." However, everyone heard "right, pitch right," except, I guess, Benny, who must have heard "right, pitch left."

I'm sure you have figured it out already. Benny pulled to his blind side and Arthur pulled right. Directly behind me, I was the center, I heard two loud grunts as the two guards collided. Now I'm sure you're thinking the play was a bust, maybe even lost yardage as two blockers were on the ground after blocking each other and not blocking anyone on the opposition—wrong.

The opponents two inside linebackers collided in front of me (both were keying on the guards to determine the way the play was going, which was a pretty standard key for inside linebackers). That collision freed me to go through the defense and get a kick out block on the outside linebacker from an unexpected angle (the linebacker was expecting a wham block from one of the pulling guards). My block sprung D.K. Porterfield for a sixty-yard scamper into the end zone.

At the Monday afternoon skull session where we reviewed the film of the game, I suggested to the coaching staff that we incorporate the play with our guards blocking each other into our playbook. The entire team laughed as Coach reran the film over and over—because I was a smart ass, I ran ten hard laps around the practice field after practice on Tuesday. See, I told you Coach didn't like me.

It was so ingrained in each member of our team to block on every play that "phantom" or "ghost" blocking was bound to occur. As I said earlier, we had very few pass plays. In fact, we only passed out of desperation. Playing our arch rivals, fourth quarter, two minutes left, down one touchdown was a desperate moment.

"Right, screen left" was the call. Now this intricate pass play, hardly ever practiced, required the weak side guard and end (remember we were unbalanced—that's our line not our players) plus the center to fake pass blocking and then wander into the left flat, not crossing the line of scrimmage, and set a screen for our tailback. Our tailback, who also had feigned a block on the onrushing defensive players, would also wander into the flat to receive a pass from the QB. The QB was "shitting his pants" trying to avoid all of the unblocked defensive players who had purposefully been brush blocked and freed up to literally murder the QB, who would loft a soft pass to the tailback.

When the tailback caught the pass, he would fall in behind the three-man screen and proceed up field. The play worked perfectly, Pat Ferrell, our end, took out the defensive corner on the left and Arthur Adkins got the safety. All that was left was clear sailing to the end zone. But wait, everyone is expected to block on each play, so, as D.K. Porterfield, the tailback following behind his beloved center passed the hometown cheerleaders his beloved center threw a ghost block (no opponent was within 20 yards of the block and ball carrier) and rolled into the middle of eight adoring "babes" for hugs and kisses.

Next Tuesday the beloved center was doing ten more hard laps around the practice field for once again being a smart ass—I told you Coach didn't like me and certainly couldn't take a joke. Although we tied our arch rivals on the "phantom" screen play, or was that the phantom block on the perfect screen play, the opponents came back in the last minute of the game and kicked a field goal to win the game. Although I laugh about the play today, fifty years later, on that Tuesday I felt like the ass that the Coach called me—like many Americans I really hate to lose!

Chapter 10
Meanest Man

*The meanest man in the (neighborhood,
town, state)… Every family has one*

Bruce Allen was my great uncle and he was known as the meanest, nastiest man in the county. Uncle Bruce would fight anyone and everyone at his truck stop along Route 3 in southern West Virginia.

Bruce's favorite way to fight was to allow his opponent to kick him as hard as they wanted in the stomach and then Bruce would get a turn to kick the opponent in the stomach, first one to fall was the loser. Most who took on the fight figured that the first kick, theirs, would send Uncle Bruce to the floor and win the fight.

No one could remember anyone beating Uncle Bruce. The fear I saw in the eyes of opponents when they had their turn and Bruce Allen was still standing was as horrifying a sight as any I have ever witnessed.

I've heard it told that you really don't need many friends in your life; only six will do, as long as they can carry your casket to your grave site. When Bruce Allen died his wife was concerned that no one would come to the funeral, and most everyone felt Bruce Allen had no friends at all.

Other than family, which included me, a recent Army OCS graduate—you know, a "shaved tail dumb-assed second lieutenant"—my brother and some other family members were all that were expected (Aunt Anne Allen had even had trouble finding a minister to preach the funeral).

Unbelievably, about 25 other people showed up. Most were men, and in the same age group as Uncle Bruce, and more unbelievably, when the sermon concluded, six old men came forward, picked up the casket, took it to the hearse and later moved it reverently to the grave site.

Who are those guys, I asked once the service was concluded? They're veterans, my dad told me. "But Dad, I know two of those guys have been in 'kicking fights' with Uncle Bruce, and some of the others have expressed nothing but hatred for Bruce." All that was true, but more important that day was Bruce Allen was a World War I combat survivor, he had served honorably in the U.S. Marine Corps and he was remembered, he was respected and he was honored, for his service to this nation and for protecting our freedoms.

I learned a valuable lesson that hot day in May of 1968. You see, I had no history of military service running through my family. To my knowledge, since the Civil War, no Callaham or Carden, or Hedrick or Davidson had served in the uniformed services of this nation until my brother joined the Navy in 1963. The first I ever heard about Uncle Bruce—married to my grandmother's sister—and his military service was at his burial.

The lesson: Even a man with few friends should always be honored and remembered for his service to his country—a code of honor and respect that I follow today. It's more important what you were—a person who has served this country, than who you were—even if you were the meanest nastiest man in the county.

Chapter 11
In-Laws

Each day of our lives we make deposits
in the memory banks of our children.
—Charles R. Swindoll

Irene passed away several years ago—tough old bird, 95 years old, she was my mother-in-law and the last of the "backstops" for my family. She and her husband Lew were the ultimate last line of defense when my generation messed up—such is the role of good parents. My parents, Arnold and Blanche, and they were good parents also, passed away nine days apart in July of 1983 leaving Lew and Irene to watch out for my wife Ruth Anne, me, their daughter Sue, husband Dan and son Don, wife Darlene.

I want to tell you about Lew and Irene, not because they were perfect or typical, but, because they personified parenting, the good and bad, for the "baby boomers' generation. To do that telling I'm thankful for the eulogy, written and delivered by Lew and Irene's daughter Sue. I've shortened it to fit the style of this book, and hopefully left enough for you to understand the American family, as I see it, as it should be.

Thank you for coming to celebrate the life of Irene Dunn Cardwell. Today we not only lay to rest a woman who touched all our lives, we say a final farewell to a beloved generation of our family.

A generation Tom Brokaw dubbed The Greatest Generation; a generation for which hard work was the norm. A generation for which duty and honor were not attributes to aspire to, they were just part of their lives because it was the right way to live. They struggled through the Great Depression, helped to defeat tyranny worldwide and then built this country to greatness. … My dear siblings and cousins—we are now 'The older generation.'

It was quite a journey for Irene. From a little girl sitting on the floor in rural Kentucky, playing with her paper dolls cut out of a catalog to single handedly taking three small children halfway around the world to live in Germany. … How did she get there?

Well, when she graduated from high school, her parents wanted her to continue her education. But it was 1938. Her family had spent years living one place then another, sometimes with relatives, after her father lost his store. Her talented seamstress mother had difficulty selling quilts. In fact, her grandma Mattie used her egg money to buy the fabric for Irene's white graduation dress. Obviously, college was out of the question. So, her parents sent her to the big city—to Louisville—to live with her aunt and used their small savings to send her to business school.

The family next door to her aunt seemed nice enough, but night after night Irene was awakened by the sound of the family's son pulling into the driveway well after midnight. 'Great' she thought, 'I had to move next door to a playboy.' She wondered if he even slept because his car was always gone when she left in the morning.

Then one Sunday evening, Rodney, a nice boy from church asked her to the church social. Since Rodney didn't a have car, so they went on the bus, which was fine with Irene. She loved everything about living in the big city, except maybe being awakened every night by the playboy next door.

Irene and Rodney were standing together at the social when she noticed out of the corner of her eye someone coming toward them. Wonderful—it was the playboy. He introduced himself, 'Hi, I'm Lew Cardwell.' The three of them talked for a while. Lew, known to his family as Rollie, telling stories, making them laugh. Finally, he offered them a ride home. Since Irene lived next door, Lew took Rodney home first. Then Lew asked Irene if she wanted to stop for a White Castle. That was their first date and the beginning of a never dull 63 years together.

After that night she couldn't go to sleep until she heard him pull in the drive and knew he was home safe. Mom was a worrier. She worried about everyone she loved for her whole life.

How to describe Mom. She grew up in a family where there was very little conversation and almost no laughter. And a lot of restrictions. Although her mother was a gentle soul, there was little physical display of affection and no talk of loving each other.

But Lew let the little bird out of her cage! For the first time Irene was wearing makeup. She learned to dance (and found she loved dancing, dressing up, going to parties and having parties). She played cards for the first time; drank Coca Cola for the first time; wore a swim suit for the first time. She had her first drink and smoked her first cigarette, although she never did either of those very much. She went to movies. I believe John Dunn always regretted sending his daughter off to the city.

But she was still a very shy person who married into a raucous family, full of talk, stories, games and laughing, not to mention practical jokes. She loved watching the fun and being near it, but seldom felt confident enough to join in.

During her life she lived in eleven states and two countries. Kentucky was always home, but she was mighty partial to Texas.

If I had to select one word to describe mom, I believe I would choose 'strong.' She was always willing to get out of her comfort zone. It can be quite daunting to be athletically challenged in an athletically gifted family.

Also, mom was never completely comfortable flying in small aircraft, but as you all know, she did fly in several of them many, many times. And when Daddy said that, as a safety matter, she needed to learn to land the plane—she learned to land the plane.

Mom learned that first night at White Castle that Daddy was in fact not a playboy. He came home late at night and left early in the morning because he had two, sometimes three jobs, as he had since he was eight years old and would have most of his life.

We all know Daddy was bigger than life. I wonder if it occurred to anyone that in order for him to get his high school diploma after leaving school to help support the family; earn Bachelor's and Master's degrees; serve as Master of his Lodge and a member of numerous other organizations; fly his plane; travel Monday through Friday for one job; work nights and weekends on two more jobs; and raise three children … someone had to have his back. That someone was mom. Mom checked the spelling and grammar on his essays (before we had computers to do that), called the repairmen, kept the second car running, met our school needs, fed us, bought our clothes and worked full time to help support the family.

When the military sent Daddy to a new assignment, or when he moved to a new location for a promotion, mom oversaw the packing and shipping of household goods, discontinued utilities and closed the house while he went on ahead. She was a 'Super Mom' before anyone coined that term.

Strong is definitely the right word. In the last eleven years mom overcame a lot. She lost her husband of 63 years, had open heart surgery, two broken hips, pneumonia, a pulmonary embolism, etc. She overcame it all. Every time, she got up out of bed, went back to using her walker, fixing herself meals, took only one pill a day (how many of us would like to say that) and most importantly—she went to have her hair done every Friday morning!

Then five weeks ago Mom broke one small bone in her foot. And it was just too much. I believe that last Tuesday, before a new day dawned, Daddy came to her, took her hand and said 'Come on Renie. It's time to go—the children will be all right; we raised them well.'

Now she has returned to where she began. There's an old lullaby that goes in part: "You are mighty lucky/ Babe of old Kentucky/ close

your eyes in sleep/Fly away Kentucky Babe/fly away to rest/Close your eyes in sleep."
Good night Mom.

What more can I write? There are many lessons about parenting in this eulogy for all of us—I hope you find at least one!

Chapter 12
Wife

*Happy is the man who finds a true friend, and far happier
is he who finds that true friend in his wife.*
—Franz Schubert

*Good girls go to heaven; redheads go where
ever they damn well please!*
—pagecovers.com

In this section of the book, I saved the best chapter until last—
this chapter is about my wife.

Ruth Anne Cardwell was twenty, a senior at Southwest Texas
State University (L.B.J.'s alma mater), slim, trim, witty and a
redhead. I first saw her coming into the Raven Room in the Fort
Sam Houston Officers' Club. I think I fell in love with her that
very moment.

She, on the other hand took her time before she gave away
her heart to a twenty-one-year-old Second Lieutenant, college
dropout (flunkout is a better word) with little future other than
a guaranteed trip to Southeast Asia. However, by the ninth of
October, a year and a half later, both hearts were joined and have
stayed that way for fifty years.

Ruth Anne's life has been eclectic in many ways: She was born
in Kentucky and reared in Texas, while also living in Germany,

Virginia, Illinois, Maryland and finally back in Texas. Along the way she's been a NASA researcher, a pharmaceutical company technician, a student (MBA from Mount Saint Mary's University and educational doctoral work at the University of Virginia), a mother (bore two children and raised them well with little help from me), a communications and computer specialist with the Department of Defense and the Internal Revenue Service, the director of a regional not-for-profit food bank, a test examiner for the Office of Personnel Management, a lab technician for a medical laboratory, a teacher (at high schools, colleges and universities), an elected school board member, a candidate for city council and finally an elected county commissioner—slept little and loved her husband; she always has "had my back" and I've always had hers.

By herself she is awesome; together as a team we've even been better. Although she tires easily from being together so much, I believe she still looks forward to tackling the problems of life in a cooperative and coordinated manner. Would she have chosen a different path to go anywhere she pleased? I expect so. However, I also feel that she has enjoyed the path we have traveled together.

I like to use sports analogies to make my point; Ruth Anne is the player on the team that wants the ball when the game is on the line. Sure, she has made the shot that won the game and sometimes she has missed the mark, but her competitive bent always brings her back to play. A positive outlook, strong faith, and the aggressiveness that goes with being a redhead are her personal traits, and I for one wouldn't have it any other way.

I love you Ruth Anne, always have and always will.

Section 2

FRIENDS

Don't be dismayed by goodbyes. A farewell is necessary before you can meet again. And meeting again, after moments or lifetimes, is certain for those who are friends.

——Richard Bach

Since there is nothing so well worth having as friends, never lose a chance to make them.

——Francesco Guicciardini

Friends, and I like to think I have many, are the glue that holds relationships together. If your wife is not your best friend then you probably need to find a new wife, or at least work on developing a best friend relationship with the one you have. Same goes for husbands.

The best business relationships are based on friendship, at least that's my take on business. Competition is great when it's friendly and worst when its cutthroat. Having friends in high places, and even some in low places, is a good way to travel along the highways and byways of life.

There is nothing sadder than having no friends. Who ya' gonna turn to? And *Ghostbusters* is not a realistic answer. Really, where do you turn if you have no friends? Of course, "family" is one answer, but when family is not an option for any number of reasons, then it's good to have friends.

So, my encouragement parallels Guicciardini's stated above: Never lose a chance to make friends!

Chapter 1
Relationships

Friends fund friends.
—Richard F. Trump, candidate for mayor,
City of Hagerstown Maryland, January 2005

I'm sure many people, some even famous, stated that "friends fund friends." I, however, heard it first from Richard F. (Dick) Trump. So, he gets credit for the quote. Interestingly enough, that quote and its manifestation in practice in the noted city election came back to haunt not only Dick, but the folks who ran as a team of candidates in that now (by my standards) infamous election—more on that later in another story.

Americans fully understand the quote in its broader context—broader than the money implication. Whether it is talking politics or even something as simple as a not-for-profit fundraiser, or a bank loan, or sale of property, or a marriage, or the chance meeting of a stranger in a business office, or even a legal dispute—it is the "relationship" that must come first. And that relationship must be at least friendly.

In this day and age where the handshake doesn't mean as much as it used to, the adage of "friends fund friends" has lost some of its luster. For example, recently a lady at my doctor's office, while she was looking frantically for a phone number for the local taxi company, asked me for a ride to the downtown—where I was going. My radar went up, and feelings of being taken advantage of immediately came to my mind—legal implications, violent crime, rape, false accusation, my reputation—I refused the lady the ride. I used some lame excuse (most Americans call that lying) that I was going in the opposite direction. In the same instance I totally forgot all those September, October and November nights, after high school football practice, hitchhiking home on lonely deserted roads in rural West Virginia. In those days "friends fund friends" simply meant a safe ride home.

Americans review relationships on an individual basis, realizing that all friendships do not have to be intimate, personal or touchy or long-standing. Rather, friendships can be instantaneous or spontaneous and often have nothing to do with money. To renew our faith in one another, many Americans will take some risk to recognize friendship opportunities and renew the luster of friends fund friends. (I went back in the doctor's office found the lady and drove her downtown, because that's what an American should do.)

Chapter 2
Pride

You got to have pride, son.
—Carroll Reid, head football coach, Smithburg High School,
1991 (at least that was the first time I heard Coach Reid utter those
words.)

This vignette is about leaders and leadership, but before I begin let me give you a little background surrounding one of the sources I am using.

I have a passion for reading. In fact, when I entered school at Central Elementary in Hinton, West Virginia, my mother, who later retired after forty-plus years as a high school teacher, suggested to my first-grade teacher: "Teach my son to read, because if he can read, he can master anything." Reading has been an integral part of my life for all of these years, and yes, like mom predicted, I have mastered a few things.

My choice of reading material is eclectic, everything from newspapers, periodicals, trade journals, pulp and trash novels, scientific journals and blogs to history books, including historical fiction. Historical fiction is my favorite. Among the many authors I follow regularly is Bernard Cornwell. Cornwell has written many books including several series. The Sharpe novels may be the best known. Along with the Sharpe novels, I am fond of *The Saxon Tales*. Those tales chronicle the exploits of the fictional "Uhtred of Bebbanburg," stylized according to Cornwell, "his blood is

Saxon, his heart is Viking and his battleground is England." The tales take place during the time of the very real King Alfred, circa 850-900 A.D. I'm sure you get the picture.

In a recent tale Cornwell, through Uhtred, provides the following synopsis about leaders and leadership: "It is not difficult to be a lord, a jarl, or even a king, but it is difficult to be a leader. Most men want to follow … They must be led … They must be surprised and challenged; given tasks they think beyond their abilities. And they must fear … but fear is not enough. They must love, too … then a man who loves his leader will fight better than a man who merely fears him. At that moment we are brothers, we fight for each other, and a man must know that his leader will sacrifice his own life to save any one of his men."

Carroll Reid was a leader. He was both feared and loved and his boys formed a brotherhood under his leadership on the football field. Most felt that Reid would sacrifice anything to help his boys win. "You got to have pride" he would bellow when he wanted to inspire or love them—or the antithesis: "you got no pride," to invoke a sense of fear.

Reid literally started the football program at Smithsburg High School and over the course of forty years, including time off to be treated for Hodgkin's disease, became the second winningest coach in the State of Maryland by the time he retired. All of that at a tiny 1A (lowest category in Maryland high school rankings) school located in the western part of Maryland. Along the way he won four state football titles.

But leadership doesn't always mean victory. In the summer of 1991 (his junior year in high school) my son decided to play football; I became a more than proud Smithsburg football parent. You see, I played football as a kid in West Virginia, almost played at the college level and have had a life-long passion for the game. My son, until the summer of 1991, had shown little interest in playing the game—basketball, not football was his forte.

But during the summer of '91 a good friend (who later became a Maryland state trooper) encouraged my son to play football for Coach Reid because "Coach will teach you about pride." And Reid did—my son, now an Episcopal priest, frequently recalls Reid's lessons, Reid's passion for winning and Reid's passion to instill pride in his players. Reid simply believed that overcoming the difficulties associated with tasks that were perceived to be "beyond their abilities" meant having pride. Pride in oneself.

Wilde Lake was a "technical high school," based on Maryland's standards at the time. Although their student population was in the category of 4A schools (Maryland's highest category), in 1991 Wilde Lake was still categorized as a 1A school (don't ask me to explain). In 1992, Wilde Lake would graduate four football players who would go on to play Division 1 football in college—simply stated, this team was loaded with all-star talent.

In the November 1991 USA Today high school football rankings, Wilde Lake was the Number 4 team in the nation. During the 1991 season, Wilde Lake went 10-0 with an average victory margin of 30-plus points per game. Several of their impressive wins were against 4A schools. During the playoffs, Wilde Lake was 2-0 and these victories included a 37-point win in the state quarterfinals, and an impressive 30-point win in the semis. Wilde Lake was slated to meet Smithsburg High School in the 1A State Football Championship game.

That same season Smithsburg was 9-1, losing to a powerful Middletown team that ultimately won the State 2A Championship. (Interestingly enough, Smithsburg probably could have won that Middletown game, but in the second quarter, Smithsburg's middle linebacker tackled Middletown's fullback and fractured the young man's neck. This event seemed to take the wind out of Smithsburg's sails and the Leopards succumbed to the Knights by 7 points.) Going 2-0 in the playoffs, Smithsburg had a much harder time than Wilde Lake winning each game by 7 or less points. Smithsburg was clearly no pushover, but on paper appeared out of their league against Wilde Lake.

Halftime in the championship game found the score knotted at 7. Taking the second half kickoff, Wilde Lake easily marched 60 yards and scored, missing the extra point to go up 13-7. Reid called time out.

"You got to have pride, boys. You're tired, you're outgunned and outmanned, but you've got more pride than those boys! Now go out there and play the rest of this game for your pride!" Smithsburg took the ensuing kickoff and moved the ball down the field and nearly scored, finally being stopped at the Wilde Lake 10-yard line on downs.

Over the next twelve minutes, the teams moved back and forth drawing no blood. Then suddenly in the fourth quarter, Wilde Lake's all-state halfback bucked into the middle of the offensive and defensive lines; Smithsburg's middle linebacker filled the hole. The outcome of these two powerful titans colliding looked like a rugby scrum. Just like in rugby, one player emerged with the ball and raced to the other team's goal—it was Toby Williams, Smithsburg's middle linebacker. The score was 14-13 Smithsburg up by one.

Smithsburg kicked off and held Wilde Lake to a three-and-out, forcing a punt. Wilde Lake's punt was downed inside the Smithsburg 10-yard line. Less than two minutes left in the game, Smithsburg ran three plays and lost five yards, forcing them to punt.

One minute left, Smithsburg punted—Wilde Lake blocked it and scored, winning the game 19-14. Smithsburg had lost, but just the game, not their pride. Carrol Reid summed it up to me in a conversation I had with him just before he passed on. He said, "I've never been prouder after a game than I was after the Wilde Lake game. We should have lost by 30 or more. But the boys played their hearts out, they played for pride, they played to accomplish something no one else thought they could."

Americans know that there is victory even in defeat if you give your all, do your best, leave it all on the field of play. To this day, I know several of the young men who played for Reid that year (including, of course, my son). To a person they all recall his leadership, his pride, his love for the game and for "his boys." These are lessons for us all to learn.

Chapter 3
Friendship

The one thing I've learned about friends
is that the good ones are rare.
—Lauren Conrad

I made a fool of myself the other day, which seems to happen more frequently as I grow older. I stood in front of my Rotary Club and tried to say something profound about Claud Kitchens, who had recently passed on, and with a huge lump in my throat, all I could do was stand there and weep quietly.

Claud Kitchens was a long-standing Rotarian, retired superintendent of public schools in our county, and above all else he was my friend.

Oh, I wasn't crying for Claud, you see, my faith reminds me that the good ones go on to a better place—and make no mistake Dr. Claud Estes Kitchens Jr. was one of the very good ones. No, I cried for myself because I had lost a good friend, a mentor and neighbor. I cried for all of the Rotarians in the room—even the ones who didn't know him—because they also had lost a friend. And finally, I cried for all of the folks in Washington County, their children and children's children, because we had lost a great community friend and educator.

One of my Rotarian buddies smiled as he read from Claud's obituary: Claud earned a reputation on the basketball court at the University of South Carolina as a "cool, calculating piece of long-range artillery." Who else but Claud Kitchens could bear that fearsome reputation while being the epitome of civility with parents of school children and sensitive even to a lonely six-year-old brought to the principal's office for discipline? Claud was quite a man!

I hope my friend Lou Scally will not be mad at me for retelling one more apropos moment relating to our friend Claud. About ten minutes after I played the fool, Lou approached me to brighten my mood. He related that a week or so before, he saw Claud, slapped him on the back and said, "Congratulations on having that school (Fairview) named after you, you know they usually don't do that until you pass on." To which Claud replied with his quick smile and a wink acknowledging Lou's caring thought.

Lou then went on to quickly say to me, "I know how you feel, Art, I will miss Claud too, and particularly just the way (in that genuine southern drawl) he said the word 'school'." How appropriate Lou, Dr. Claud E. Kitchens Jr. and "school" in the same thought.

God bless you Claud, and may God continue to bless us all with knowing the "good ones" like you. Americans will understand these sentiments.

Chapter 4
Grantland Rice

*For when the One Great Scorer comes to write
against your name, He marks not that you won
or lost, but how you played the game.*

—Henry Grantland Rice

Not everything in sports revolves around the big three: football, basketball and baseball; sometimes riding a bicycle as a volunteer can bring about visions of sporting heroics.

The sporting venue was the famous C&O Canal; the length of the pitch was 184 miles; the time clock was set to one day; the trophy was a healthy donation to a local food bank to buy food for children.

My apologies to the famous sportswriter Grantland Rice whose prose I willingly admit to using and paraphrasing.

Outlined in the dark of a hot July morning stood two horsemen, not the famous four from the sacred word, not the four from the Notre Dame backfield. These two were neither death nor destruction, nor famine nor pestilence, but rather "grit" and "gall." Their real names are Dan and Mike. Rather than facing the Nebraska line or Fordham's Seven Blocks of Granite, Grit and Gall had to muster the tenacity and endurance to ride 184 miles from the Queen City (Cumberland, Maryland) past the Great Falls to the land of spin (Washington, D.C.)—a daunting task notwithstanding the hot air at the beginning and the end.

"All wars are planned by old men in council rooms apart" and such was the war with the trail. Grit and Gall were ready at the call and chose not the noble Equus Ferus caballus to ride, but rather sleek graphite two-wheeled foot powered machines that break the wind and carry their riders at unheard of speeds.

"The children are hungry and many are down on their luck" was the rallying cry. No bridge too far or tunnel too dark would keep these champions of the downtrodden from their appointment with lasting gratitude and local fame.

The canal was like a cyclone full of twists and curves, wheel deep with mud from a recent rain, and everyone knows that "a cyclone can't be snared." It may be surrounded, but somewhere it breaks through to keep even the most experienced from going on. When the cyclone starts in Cumberland, where the candle lights still gleam through the Maryland pines, those in the way must give up the ride, take to storm cellars at top speed and wait for the weather to break. Not Grit and Gall! When the cyclone roared, Grit and Gall roared back, heads down, eyes fixed on the prize, and with vinegar in their piss the two horsemen rode on.

Dan and Mike were adept at broken field cycling, yet on this day they found few chances to even get started. You can figure the cyclone's strength is barricading the road and Grit and Gall had to find new ways to navigate the rough road. The canal is one road that is hard to suppress, but Grit and Gall found a few chances to show their broken-field ability. You can't run through a broken field unless you get there, and get there they did.

Well, enough is enough, my personal thanks and the thanks of the food bank, its board, donors and clients, to Dan and Mike for their fundraiser that raised over one thousand dollars to help the local community.

One final tribute to Grantland Rice that may be little more than faint praise for Dan and Mike's noteworthy accomplishment:

"Does the road wind uphill all the way? Yes, to the very end. Will the day's journey take the whole long day? From morn to night, my friend." Thanks for riding uphill all day for this community. Americans "who have tackled a cyclone will understand."

Chapter 5
Widow's Mite

And He looked up and saw the rich putting their gifts into the treasury, and He saw also a certain poor widow putting in two mites.
—The Gospel of Luke

One of my very good friends asked me to write about God's economy. So, let me do a disclaimer and try to be as politically and religiously correct as possible. I'll call this "The Superpower's Economy."

As I will freely admit, I am a Christian in terms of my religious conviction, and the Superpower that I'm writing about I refer to as God. I hope that what I write about though is applicable to each and every person. I know that many have other religious persuasions and some probably contend they are not religious at all. Therefore, I have chosen this innoxiously generic name—Superpower—to be all inclusive for believers of different faiths and nonbelievers alike.

The friend, who asked me to write about God's economy, the Reverend Anne Weatherholt, preached a sermon that she titled: *The Sermon on the A-mount*. I was touched by her remarks (many I have used and paraphrased below). Later at lunch with Anne I explored her thesis and saw that thesis fits well in my efforts to write about economies and Americans. We know and talk about the local, national and world economies, but isn't there even a higher economy where we as human beings fit? I think so.

Who has not heard of the widow's mite? This phrase has become one of our common English figures of speech. The widow's mite refers to the sum of money given by a widow to God (her Superpower) in contrast to the opulence shown by some rich folks eager for all to see their wealth.

There are some cultural facts about this story that are particularly relevant at the time the story is first related in the Christian Bible. A man's goods, upon his death, often returned to his own family which was obligated to take in his widow and support her, whether they wanted to or not. A widow could not work, so any money she might have would have been given to her, or possibly saved from her dowry.

At the time of the story the widow's nation and community were oppressed; literally all she had to live for was her Superpower. In the story, the widow, out of her poverty, contributed everything she had, her whole living to her Superpower's economy.

The word "living" in Greek is *bios,* from which we get the words biosphere, biology, biopsy, all referring to living things. This woman had contributed all of which would have otherwise gone for essential, life-giving sustenance. She gave her all, her living, as a gift.

The traditional interpretation of this story has centered on the relativity of the widow's contribution. The amount she gave was small in comparison to the amount given by others. But in relative terms, she gave proportionately more.

But if we leave the story as only a story about the "a-mount," we miss the bigger story. Think about it! The widow contributed her whole living, her whole *bios.* Clearly this is more than a lesson in generosity.

It has been said that if we were to place a price on the chemicals that make up our mortal bodies, the actual value is under $5.

Our value is truly only measured as what we do with our lives—what we give as a gift with our lives to others. It is the giving that creates the value.

The late great actor Jimmy Stewart, or if you will, the late Brigadier General, U.S. Air Force (Retired) Jimmy Stewart (twenty combat sorties during WWII), summed up what gifts he wanted to be remembered for. He said he wanted to be remembered as man of God, a good family man, and a good citizen of this great nation and his community. Stewart prioritized those things that were important in his life, those things, like the widow, to which he would contribute his life, his living.

As I pondered the story of the widow's mite, Anne Weatherholt's sermon and Jimmy Stewart's statement, I thought about all of us. To what are we willing to contribute our living as a gift? For the biblical-era widow, it was her last two coins. For us today it's our lives that are worth about $5. All the widow had was her God, her Superpower, to coin my words. Today we each have our own concept of a Superpower, which in most cases is our families, our nation and our community—four pretty good economies in which to contribute our living.

Americans understand contributing our all for the good of others. If you don't believe me, just stand in front of the Vietnam Memorial and you'll see the names of many who did.

Chapter 6
Boxing

Rhythm is everything in boxing. Every move
you make starts with your heart, and that's
in rhythm or you're in trouble.

—Ray Robinson

He started it. One night in the Teen Club, a basement level hangout for teenagers in the downtown, he asked the coach to teach him something about the "sweet science." See, the school bully was pushing him around and he wanted to be able to defend himself.

Buck suggested, "Someone bring the bully down here tomorrow night and I'll use him for practice and show you a thing or two." Most of us were afraid that the bully would hurt the Coach; Coach was in his 50's and the bully was an 18- or 19-year-old punk. Punk yes, but a thug also. He was the scourge of the after-school bus line (lately the bully wasn't even attending school, yet he showed up after last bell to terrorize the unsuspecting students) and had been the scariest thing on many playgrounds for over ten years.

So, it was on. One of the bully's few friends put out the challenge: "basement, Teen Club, Friday night, six o'clock, someone says he's going to kick your ass." The bully couldn't refuse such a kind invitation and he figured the only ass that was going to be kicked was whoever was stupid enough to call him out.

ART CALLAHAM

The bully came through the door to the club right on time and headed straight for a group of kids. But the Coach cut him off. "Old man, get out of my way 'cause I'm going to kick someone's ass and if you try to stop me, I'll kick yours too."

"OK punk, but kick mine first—and by the way, let's put on some gloves I brought tonight—don't want you to hurt your hands."

The bully got this weird look on his face, part confusion and part suspicion. Coach just donned his gloves, handed a pair to the bully and asked all the customers to form a circle around them. "So, I won't be able to run away," grinned the Coach.

For the next 10 minutes Coach gave a continuous verbal lesson about boxing to all of us in the circle while blocking every one of the bully's punches and landing many short jabs and an occasional right hook. The bully became more and more frustrated, particularly when he began to bleed. Finally, he threw down his gloves and left the club (rather quickly) in a huff. Let's have a boxing team!

That's the backdrop—a month later three other young men and I were in Coach's car heading to Mt. Hope for the Golden Gloves State Tournament. All of us were entered in the "novice" level (for those who had never fought in Golden Gloves). One was a lightweight, the two other guys were middleweights and weighing in at 203 pounds, I was fighting as a heavyweight.

Before I get to the night of the fights, let me describe my boxing attire. I had an old bathrobe that Coach's wife had dyed red, although after two or three washings it was pink at best. My boxing trunks consisted of an old pair of black swimming trunks with the lining removed, a jock strap and a cup. And topping off the ensemble (really bottoming off) was my new pair of black high-topped Chucks laced up with bright red shoestrings.

Now the lower boxing divisions had upper and lower parameters based on weight, but the heavyweight division had

82

only a lower limit—190 pounds. The lower divisions fought early and the heavyweights were the last into the ring. I drew the third heavyweight match with only one to follow. If you won you returned in a week for the semis with the finals in two weeks.

I was 16 and a junior in my high school, played football and participated in most sports. My junior year my playing weight on the football team was around 210, so on this February evening I had trimmed down to 203. I vividly remember hopping into the ring and grabbing the ropes and doing my best Sugar Ray Robinson imitation, dancing and doing deep knee bends off the ropes. Getting my rhythm on.

In the middle of my second or third knee bend the crowd erupted in cheers and loud clapping—not for me. Entering the ring was the biggest Black man I had ever seen (not really, since I had played against him in football during the fall). He was a really big man—300 pounds of muscle if he weighted an ounce.

I was the center on our football team and my boxing opponent was Mount Hope's middle guard (they played a 5/4 scheme with their middle guard over the center). He was a senior and would go on to play at Marshall College; he was All-State two years in football and one year, his junior year, in track and field.

Let me digress a moment and tell you about Mount Hope. In the '60s, Mount Hope's population was nearly 75 percent Black (this was before Blacks were referred to as African Americans). In the Coalfield Conference, Mount Hope was a perennial powerhouse in football, basketball and track and field. Mount Hope was one of two annual rivalries, and often only our team or their team stood in the other's way of state championships. And most of the population of our community was White—in the days of racial unrest, Blacks versus Whites was usually a hard-fought affair regardless of the sport.

In the football season, when we played Mount Hope I was able to handle my opponent through speed and technique, although every time I tried to use a blast block, he overpowered me and usually stuffed the play. He was a powerful man and when I looked across the ring I began to fear for my safety—I was scared shitless.

"Coach," I said "when he swings at me, I'm going to go down and stay down." "Good strategy," Coach replied, "I don't think you can take him." When we met in the middle of the ring for our instructions, my opponent just glared at me. Back to my corner, Coach told me, "Don't crowd him." "You got that shit right."

The bell rang and I went to the center of the ring and danced around a little. The big Black man didn't charge me, so I decided I would at least throw one punch—a short jab toward his nose. Bang, his head snapped back and he went down on his knees. The adrenaline kicked in, and instead of going to a neutral corner I rushed at him, put my left hand behind his head and, in the words of my father, cold-cocked him with a right hook.

The crowd erupted, this time with boos laced with angry calls for my head—on a platter … not a pretty sight in my mind's eye. Coach ran into the ring and covered me with my pink robe and hustled me through the ropes and out to the dressing room. The bell kept sounding and the referee was yelling "disqualification, disqualification!!!"

That's how I got my grandiose boxing record—I'm 0/0/0/1, that's no wins, no losses, no draws and one disqualification. I never got my rhythm on again. But the lesson for Americans is simply this: For most of us, the racial thing is not about hatred for one race or another, it's mostly about fear or misunderstanding. Although we as humans believe we are at the top of the animal kingdom, and as Americans we feel we are at the top of the human chain, we're still just animals. Animals are often driven by fear or a sense of misunderstanding.

I didn't then, nor do I now, hate Black people. In fact, I feared my boxing opponent because of my sense of his abilities to cause me harm, and I reacted the way I did. That's not an excuse, just a statement of fact. Americans of all races must get over the fears extenuated by racism.

Chapter 7
There Are a Lot of Jacks

My best friend is the man who in wishing
me well wishes it for my sake.
—Aristotle

More than anything else, this is a tribute to a good friend who passed on several years ago. On or around Independence Day I usually like to write about freedom, patriots, our military or veterans; this particular year I didn't. John R. "Jack" Hershey Jr. passed away on June 27 and was memorialized on July 2; I was honored to attend the memorial service. But Jack's passing put me in a funk. I don't know why, it just did.

Jack and I were friends. Oh, I wasn't his best friend, yet over a period of ten to fifteen years, I was proud to declare Jack as a friend. And like literally thousands of others, I always felt that Jack considered me a friend. That's just the way Jack was. I remember one of his birthday celebrations, Jack and Anna (his wife) literally rented Fort Ritchie (a closed military reservation in Maryland) for the day, where hundreds of his friends were welcomed to fete Jack on achieving another milestone.

I was awed as I stood for a few minutes and watched Jack greet each of his guests with a hug or a handshake, and each guest, for at least that moment, knew they were Jack's best friend. Jack knew how to make friends and also how to be a friend.

Many of those best friends can tell far more stories about Jack than I can tell, but one in particular comes to my mind. Jack owned several pieces of rental property, and on one occasion he rented a storefront to a fledgling entrepreneur. The renter was from out of town and didn't know much about the area. So, Jack wanted to do a big grand opening for the business and he invited several local dignitaries—the A-list—to attend. Me, I was on the B-list in my role as Executive Director of the Greater Hagerstown Committee.

Comes the day of the grand opening, and several of us B-listers were standing around drinking punch and eating cookies when we notice that none of the dignitaries were present. Totally undeterred, Jack hustles those present to the front of the store, makes the introductions of the new and proud owners and then looks over at me and says: "Art, come over and say a few words of welcome to these new business folks." Uhhhhh, well who could ever refuse Jack Hershey, so on behalf of the dignitaries that didn't show, I gave my standard "elevator speech" about economic development, business success and jobs.

Still undeterred, Jack calls out one of my business cohorts, Brien Poffenberger, to come forward and welcome the folks to our community on behalf of the Chamber of Commerce. Two B-list speeches made a new business owner extremely happy and welcome, and also made Jack a new life-long friend. As was related to me by many attending his memorial service, "Jack had a way (a good way) with people."

I could write for hours about Jack Hershey, but I want to relate Jack's passing to Independence Day, at least as it surfaced in my mind when I heard Jack had passed on. Fifty-six men signed the Declaration of Independence, actually on July 2, 1776 (the Declaration was approved on July 4), and in so doing pledged everything, even their own lives, to make this country free. That's pretty heavy-duty stuff!

Those 56 were the true patriots of our country. As I sat in the memorial service for Jack Hershey, I reflected on the passing of those 56 patriots who on that same day, July 2, 236 years earlier stood around a table and possibly signed their lives away to make America a freer and better place in which to live.

No, I'll not make Jack into a national patriot. However, if you consider our local community and those who would sign and pledge to make it a better place in which to live, many of us would have listed Jack among the ready, willing and able signers.

The author Thomas Harris in his best-selling 1988 novel *The Silence of the Lambs* penned one of my favorite quotes. The individual speaking was the archvillain Hannibal Lecter, and he was talking to the book's heroine Clarice Starling. Clarice, who was trailing Lecter, asked Lecter if he would "come after" her. Lecter responded: "... Clarice, the world is a better place with you in it."

As I have reflected on the passing of several of our community's best and finest, on July 2 of that year, I once again looked up and quietly paraphrased Harris: "Jack, the world was a better place, with you in it." We'll miss you.

Chapter 8
Another Jack

While we are mourning the loss of our friend,
others are rejoicing to meet him behind the veil.
—John Taylor

More about friends. My dad always told me that the toughest part of growing old was burying your friends. Friends, you know, the people you grew up with, your school chums, your buddies from your days in military service, the people you work with, the ones you respect or admire—your friends.

I've written about my heroes, and most of those folks were my friends. But recently, as I grow older, I want to pause and consider my friends. Why? Because over the years I've seen too many of my friends buried: Jack Hershey, Jack Corderman and Bill Stryker just to name three. Most who read this will not recognize these names, but the point is—friends die.

An old superstition asserts that deaths come in threes. I guess I could say that the deaths of friends always seem to come in threes, and would point to these friends that died within a week of each other. In some ways this "threesome" proves the merit of that superstition—at least for me.

I don't remember it that way, the "three's thing," when I was younger. Bobby Williams, an agile, underweight outside linebacker died in a horrible car wreck when I was in high school.

One of my best friends, D.K. Porterfield, home from the Navy on leave, died when I was in college. Stan Bossert, an Army friend died while I served in Vietnam and Roxanna Trump, a friend to so many, died while Ruth Anne and I were living in Maryland.

That "three's thing," just like growing old, seems to catch up with all of us later in life. However, I'm sure the insurance companies have a table that proves the superstition.

Those of you who read another of my vignettes know of my friendship with Jack Hershey. So, I'll not rehash the respect and admiration I had for him.

Bill Stryker may never have known that he was my friend, but I knew he was. We played a little golf together, and served on a nursing home board of directors together. I knew his wife; we sat at the bar in the club and had a "taste" in salute of who knows what—that's what friends do.

I lost track of Bill for a while and didn't know he was ill; that's not what friends do. It makes me sad that I can't keep up with friends as much as I used to. So, rest in peace Bill Stryker and know that your friends remember and miss you.

In many ways Jack Corderman was bigger than life. Circuit Court Judge Kenneth Long, in his eulogy for Jack, said "Jack lived two lives in one lifetime." That statement was a fitting tribute to Jack's largeness and the many lives he touched.

From Maryland to Palau (you pick the direction, go east or west, to get there) and points in between, Jack Corderman was known. Several years ago, Jack was speaking at a conference in "Po-dunk" Kentucky (actually it was at a conference center at Rough River State Park).

After announcing that he (Jack) was from Hagerstown, Maryland, during a break, a young red-headed man approached Jack with the query: "Do you know Art Callaham"? To which Jack Corderman replied in typical "Jack style," "wouldn't admit it if I did!" With that reply Jack made a new best friend of my wife's cousin (Cousin Chris was probably as hard-pressed to admit knowing me as was Jack).

Among his many areas of service to his fellow man, Jack was a Rotarian—to the bone. I bet he bled royal blue and gold. Jack was past president of a local Rotary Club and past district governor for that region. I remember when I was club president, I could never recite the "Four-way Test" correctly—was it first, second, third and fourth; or was it one, two, three and four. Jack knew and was always there to remind me I had said it incorrectly.

I think Jack forgave whomever it was that sent the bomb to his apartment; most of us who knew Jack know that he was good at forgiving and working to make things right for those he had aggrieved. But if the bomb-making culprit reads this book, then know that many of us would still sentence you to eternal damnation for that kind of cowardly act perpetrated on the judge.

I hope I'm over the "threes" for a while so, rest in peace Jack Corderman and may you be happier, more joyous and freer! And if you see Jack Hershey and Bill Stryker, I think you will, tell them Art said "hey."

Chapter 9
Heroes

*We few, we happy few, we band of brothers; for he
to-day that sheds his blood with me shall be my brother ...*
—William Shakespeare, *Henry V*

Did Henry V, King of England, ever say those words? Probably
not. But what a wonderful lament and motivational speech for
the English and Welsh longbow archers who became national
heroes by virtually annihilating the "flower of France" at the
Battle of Agincourt on Saint Crispin's Day in 1415.

Even the phrase "band of brothers" has recently become
synonymous with the men of Easy Company, 2nd Battalion,
506th Parachute Infantry Regiment and their heroic efforts
during World War II.

How about the "band of sisters," those lovely ladies on the U.S.
soccer team who, several years ago, heroically came from behind
to beat the Brazilian team only to lose heroically to the Japanese.
Did you see any of the post-game interviews that year? The
ladies demonstrated poise, class, humility and no blaming of one
another—all characteristics of heroes. Heroism knows no gender.

The 369th Infantry Regiment was the first all-black regiment
sent to fight in Europe during World War I. So tenacious and
valiant where these soldiers that they never had a unit member
captured, nor did they lose any ground during 191 days of

continuous fighting. The Germans reverently referred to the 369th as "Hellfighters"—"Harlem Hellfighters." The 369th was assigned to and fought with the French army; for its actions, the French government awarded the entire regiment the *Croix de Guerre*. Heroism knows no race.

Audie Murphy, barely 19 years old, became the most decorated soldier of all time during World War II, and Tom Watson, at sixty (long past the age where golfers compete with the thirty-something crowd) nearly won a sixth Open Championship several years ago. Heroism has no age limits.

James W.C. Pennington was a "fugitive slave/abolitionist from Maryland (who) became an internationally recognized leader of the antebellum abolitionist movement, and his work helped lay the foundation for the contemporary civil rights movement." Author Christopher Webber recounts this slave to freeman story in his book *American to the Backbone: The Life of James W.C. Pennington*. Heroism knows no station in life and is never constrained or conditioned by geography. There are heroes everywhere and in every time.

There are heroes among us or have been among us yesterday and today. Most of you readers will not recognize any or few of the following: Don and the late Joan Bowman, Coach Jim Brown, the late Mike Callas, the late Spence Perry, Wayne Alter, Ed Lough, Betty Morgan, John League, Don Munson, Mary Baykan, Joe Tischer, Emily Seidel, Harry Reynolds, the late Kevin Lumm, the late Nick Adenhart, Monty Montgomery, Nikki Houser, the late Will Taylor, Jim Latimer, Bill Barton, Tom Newcomer, Bob Cirincione, Jim Pierne, Mike Busch, Mike Miller and more—but these are but some of my personal heroes. I am remiss in not naming all of my heroes; the folks that through their lives, or even in death have painted a picture of heroism in my eyes. This vignette is short and my list is long. (See Appendix A for a longer list)

Heroes inspire, motivate, build a sense of awe within us and are role models and become the people we look up to. Most people will list their parents, their spouse, a teacher, a coach or a spiritual leader among their personal heroes. My entire list, and it is exhaustive, includes each of these categories. Most peoples' list of heroes will include names of people known only to the person who makes the list. My short list, above, has many names that many readers will not recognize, yet in my eyes they are no less heroic.

Some will read my short list and disagree with some of the names; that is everyone's right. Heroism to me is personal as well as imperfect. Personal in that one who inspires or motivates me may be disagreeable to you and others, and imperfect as well, because once a hero is not indicative of always a hero.

Recall Ira Hayes, one of the brave Americans who raised the flag atop Mount Suribachi, signifying victory in one of the bloodiest battles of World War II. The heroic moment was captured for all times in a photograph later to become the inspiration for the Marine Corps War Memorial (the Iwo Jima Monument) at Arlington National Cemetery. Hayes, a national hero, died an alcoholic, drowning in a mud puddle. His efforts, along with thousands of others, on Iwo Jima was an inspiration for future Americans going into harm's way; his death, not heroic, was a tragedy for all who know the story.

Who are your heroes? On hot summer days, over a cool glass of iced tea, it is good to ponder their names and let them inspire you again.

Section 3

WAR AND PEACE

Human beings are born for peace; they like to grow up in peace. They like to raise their children in peace, and they like to say goodbye to this beautiful life in peace. Then why are we always preparing for war?
——Debasish Mridha

To be prepared for war is one of the most effective means of preserving peace.
——George Washington

The preceding quote seems in general conflict with George Washington's quote above. I think that is the dichotomy when you contrast or compare the two concepts "war" and "peace" in a single thought. I've seen both. Oh, not war like my brothers and sisters in arms saw in WWII, Korea, Iraq, Afghanistan or others in Vietnam. Yes, I saw the elephant, but not one as large or menacing as others did—but it was war.

And not peace like the idyllic representation of the Garden of Eden before the fall; my peace is an inner peace that comes with a knowledge that my family and friends are safe. I'm no expert on war or peace, just an observer on life's highway.

The stories and opinions on the succeeding pages in this section are simply a compendium of thoughts about war and peace.

Reading these will not make war worse than it truly is, nor will it make peace better. Yet perhaps these vignettes will cause you, the reader, to contemplate your own wars and your own peacefulness with a thought toward making your life and the lives around you better.

Chapter 1
Freedom

The cost of freedom is always high,
but Americans have always paid it.
—John F. Kennedy

There are things that are precious to many Americans; this vignette is about two of those precious things—history and beer.

First a little history: My mom and dad, like most of the country of their time, called the 30th of May "Decoration Day." This was before three-day weekends and the bastardization of remembrance days to afford many of us another day off work. Oh, don't get me wrong, I enjoyed the time off, but now in my dotage I long for a simpler way to follow time and wish that the Memorial Day holiday would return to the 30th day of May.

Other than a story from Waterloo, New York, about an 1866 ceremony and parade, Memorial Day, nee Decoration Day, was inaugurated on May 30, 1868, by order of General John A. Logan, Commander of the Grand Army of the Republic. The day included the placing of wreaths (decorations) on Union and Confederate graves at Arlington Cemetery. The purpose of the day was to remember those who gave their lives during the Civil War. It wasn't until the early 1900s, after America's involvement in other wars, that most states celebrated the day of remembrance,

Southern states being the last holdouts. The day, Memorial Day, a day to remember the cost of freedom was finally, officially, recognized by Congress for the entire nation in 1966.

After World War I the red poppy became the symbol of Decoration Day, likely because of a poem penned by Moina Michael in 1918 in response to the popular John McCrea poem, "In Flanders Fields." Michael wrote:

We cherish too, the poppy red
That grows on fields where valor led,
It seems to signal to the skies
That blood of heroes never dies.

The blood of heroes, how does that relate to beer? Well, he was 33 years old at the time, Captain Donny Monn (not his real name), a member of an advisory team in Military Region 1, Republic of Vietnam. Thirty-three was old for a captain in those days. I wasn't the youngest, but I was only 22 when I was promoted to that rank. Donny had served several years as an enlisted soldier before going to Officer Candidate School and receiving a commission as an Infantry Second Lieutenant—a big demotion he would say—but then in 1971, Donny was a captain leading a Military Assistance Team on his third tour—two as an enlisted man and now a third tour as an officer.

I once wrote op-ed columns for a local newspaper, and the one I wrote ahead of Memorial Day in 2011 happened to be the 33rd I had submitted for publication. It is because of that number, 33, that I recalled Donny Monn, his life and death, for maybe the one thousandth time. Donny was a hero who shed his blood and gave his life to maintain the principles of duty, honor, country and freedom that we as Americans so revere.

Thirty-three is a lucky number to some, but not for Donny; he died of wounds he received when his camp was "underrun."

Yes, I said "underrun." His death was senseless in that the North Vietnamese units at the time, and in that area of operations, were under strict orders to not kill Americans since we were going home and "Vietnamization," a great politically correct concept, was going to keep South Vietnam free.

Donny was wearing Korean "tiger fatigues," popular with South Vietnamese Army officers, and was probably mistaken for a South Vietnamese soldier as he ran to the tower where the rest of the Americans were trying to repulse the attack. The North Vietnamese never fired a shot in anger at the tower. I am convinced that the only reason they attacked the camp was that they could. With Americans leaving and our resolve fading, their attack and victory (although they left the camp immediately after they rushed through the compound) was merely a precursor to the events that occurred over the succeeding four years that eventually led to the fall of South Vietnam. That is how 33-year-old Donny Monn died.

The number 33 also reminds me of a beer many of us drank while serving in Vietnam: "ba moui ba" or Bierre 33, as the French would say. The day after Donnie's death several Americans sat around a mortar pit and drank toasts with warm ba moui ba to the life and memory of Donny Monn. Frequently, I'll drink a beer to remember Donny and 58,310 other men and eight women, whose names appear on a simple black granite wall on the mall in Washington D.C. Every time I pass that wall, I become overcome by emotions as I remember those bitter years of fighting, both here at home and in the fields of Vietnam, because of that war.

Some Americans forgot then, and some forget now, that if not us, then who will preserve the principles of freedom for all mankind that have made us the greatest nation in the world? At least for today, in spite of the inept leadership rampant in Washington, D.C., we are still the bright shining city on the hill, the symbol to the world of what can occur when free people are willing to pay the ultimate price for the freedom of others. We are the land of the free as long as we remain the home of the brave—trite but true.

Regardless of our differing views about war today and wars of yesterday, may we, as Americans, never forget and always be willing to defend those magnificent principles—duty, honor, country and freedom. The cost of freedom is always high.

Chapter 2
Memorial

It is foolish and wrong to mourn the men who died.
Rather we should thank God that such men lived.
—General George S. Patton Jr.

"And the greatest of these is love." So says Saint Paul in his first letter to the faithful in Corinth. I am profoundly moved each year with Americans' commemorations of those who paid the ultimate price for our freedoms. These commemorations surrounding 9/11, Memorial Day and Veterans Day are days of remembrance set aside to recall those who died in harm's way.

In many ways I revel in this approach as I remember on each September 11; no, every day, those New York City fire and police members who died by cowards' hands, along with 3,000 other innocents during the events known today as 9/11. Their sacrifice of love for their fellow man was made in an undeclared war, yet that sacrifice was no less a sacrifice of love and duty to those same principles that men and women in uniform make for us today and have made for us in the past.

Every Veterans Day, and on Memorial Day each year, I also like to remember others who never wore the uniform, like my dad, who was disqualified for military service. He worked at home on the C&O Railroad to help deliver war material to factories all across our great nation.

I like to remember Rosie the Riveter who took her place on the assembly line to build the implements of war—no, implements that brought us peace—while others were off at the front.

A couple of years ago I got a new memory. Watching a TV news show, I saw the video of a man in an orange shirt unloading emergency supplies after a Midwest tornado. In some ways nothing memorable about an American doing what Americans do, helping other folks in a time of need. But now etched in my mind is the picture of that man; he only had one arm, but he was working diligently by himself to unload those supplies. It is good that such men live among us today.

I like to remember husbands, wives, mothers, fathers and all those who sent their kinfolks off to war. I cannot fathom the grief some felt when those loved ones did not return. I like to remember all those who stayed at home, never saw the rockets' red glare or felt the bombs bursting in air, yet gave a fair measure in support of our nation. This, my friend, is the manifestation of love.

Patton's timeless remark, "It is foolish and wrong to mourn the men who died; rather we should thank God that such men lived," brings me to my conclusion.

It is altogether proper that we remember the lives of all of those who have gone before us, but let us also remember those who live today and keep us free. Today and every day, let us give thanks for the lives of the men and women who serve this nation in uniforms proudly displaying the insignia of the U. S. Army, Navy, Air Force, Marines, Space Force and Coast Guard, and also those who serve as police, fire and rescue, security, and men and women who volunteer to perform those many jobs that ultimately protect our lives and our freedom.

Let every day be a Memorial Day to those who are gone, but also to those who live today and preserve the principles of duty, honor, country and freedom. Let us also remember that our greatest gift is the love we have for one another.

Chapter 3
Vietnam

*Vietnam vets who answered the call and
tried to save these people in South Vietnam
and got hammered from all sides."*
——Bill O'Reilly

I was just a "butter bar," dumb-assed second lieutenant on my first assignment, awaiting intelligence school after graduating from Officer Candidate School at Fort Belvoir, Virginia. That first assignment was as a special services officer at Fort Sam Houston, Texas. It was January of 1969; I had just turned 21 the previous October—finally old enough to die for my country and drink something other than 3.2 beers at the post exchange.

In five months, I would be promoted to first lieutenant, and in 17 months, while deployed in Vietnam, I would be promoted to captain. But on that January day I was on a plane from San Antonio, Texas, to Denver, Colorado. My express purpose in the trip was to meet up with Susan Hayes, do a little skiing and make a lot of love with the latest "girl of my dreams." I had recently met Susan at an Army Special Services conference, and although she was ten years my senior, I was infatuated with her large bosom, her straightforward approach to life ("get it while you can") and a pair of legs that went from the ground up to … well, you know where.

Promotions, my next assignment, skiing and making love were the things on my mind, and never once did I expect to be spit on. The war in Vietnam, although on every young man's mind, was tucked away in the back corners of mine. In fact, I hadn't given much thought to the war since I had skipped out of the Beckley, West Virginia, Armed Forces Enlistment Evaluation Station (AFEES) nearly two years earlier.

But there I was getting off a plane in Denver. As I proceeded through the terminal, I kept looking for Susan, who was to meet me at the airport. Off to my left that day was a group of young folks in civilian clothes carrying signs that I had paid little attention to until the spit started flying.

In those days, military personnel wearing their uniforms could fly "space-A" (space available), usually at a discount of fifty percent or more. So, I was an easy target, wearing my Class A uniform. In addition to the young men spitting, the girls were flaunting signs that read "U.S. military are baby killers" or such, while yelling "BABY KILLER" at me.

Just as I turned to confront the group, Susan grabbed my arm and pulled me down the corridor toward the exit. "Easy, easy" Susan implored. "We've got better things to do." She was right, of course, but two days later during my trip down the same corridor to catch my return flight, a short left hook and a straight right sent two agitators to the carpet as the rest ran away. "No babies killed here, just a couple of assholes on the ground," I yelled. Several travelers applauded as I made my flight, while others booed.

I learned a valuable lesson that day: Not everyone loves soldiers during unpopular wars. Many Americans found out that Rudyard Kipling was right: "… throw 'im out, the brute, but 'e's hero of 'is country when the guns begin to shoot." World War II soldiers were heroes, Korean War soldiers were forgotten and Vietnam War soldiers were labeled by some as baby killing thugs—Americans know the truth. Welcome home my brothers and sisters.

Chapter 4
Vietnam Reprise

No event in American history is more misunderstood than
the Vietnam War. It was misreported then,
and it is misremembered now.
—Richard M. Nixon

I've recounted in several of the vignettes in this book stories about war, in particular the Vietnam War. Some of the stories are based on personal experience and others are stories told by others. Some are compilations of personal knowledge and others' experiences. Like many who will read this book, I've seen the elephant; he was not so big to me as he was to others. Yet, in all of my writings, I have not been able to portray the feelings, the horror, the boredom and the exhilaration felt by the basic infantryman or marine serving "on the line."

Beyond the feelings, horror, boredom and exhilaration, I've never been able to answer the basic question about that war—a question asked by me and by most who served: "What did those who died die for?" Well, Michael Peterson, in his novel *A Time of War*, does a pretty good job of answering that question.

Before I recount some excerpts from *A Time of War*, let me give you a short background on the author. Michael Peterson has written other novels, most notably *The Immortal Dragon*, set mainly in Vietnam. He is a former Marine lieutenant who served on active duty between 1967 and 1971. Some may recall that Peterson was convicted of the murder of his second wife, appealed the guilty verdict, and at a second trial entered an Alford Plea of manslaughter, and was sentenced to time served and freed. His personal life aside, his writing is, I believe, excellent, and his fictional description of events "on the line" jells with other accounts from trusted sources who were there.

I've read Tom Clancy and Ralph Peters, along with *Platoon* and *We Were Soldiers Once, and Young,* among many books about many wars. I've watched far too many war movies and television series, and have been unable to come up with a better answer than Peterson's. So, I'll include a few excerpts on several subjects before the answer.

About war in general, the horror and exhilaration:

He shuddered at the feeling quaking through him. Then he laughed out loud and he said, "Hopeless."

Bishop turned respectfully, "What is, sir?"

He didn't speak for a long time, then he said, "I was thinking about war, Lieutenant."

"Yes, sir?"

"It's an awful thing. Oh, God, the suffering and misery ..." In his mind he saw the frozen dead at Chosin, and the bloated dead on the beach a Guadalcanal.

And Bishop saw in his mind the dead lying at his feet, and Miller's severed head and he said, "Yes, sir, it is."

Marshall turned to him. "But the truly awful thing is that ... you love it and would go back in a minute."

Bishop had not expected that, but smiled. "That's what the gunny says—though not quite in those words; it was something about war being like his first wife, and how both could stiffen your dick."

Marshall laughed. *"Well, there it is, God's very own truth spoken through the mouth of a Marine gunnery sergeant."* Then he shook his head sadly. *"Dear God, what a curse on us."* He sighed. *"And our children."*

About race relations:

Race too was a problem, but again not on the line.
'I can call Williams a nigger out here on the hill,' Sutherland said, "and he can call me a redneck motherfucker, and it's okay, 'cause we got bigger problems to worry about—like the gooks blowing our fucking heads off. But in the rear, we'd be real respectful to one another, or else we'd square off in a second."

And now the question and an answer:

"Sir, my best buddy got killed ... I want to know why he died. I want to know if he died for anything."
... "I'm going to give you the most terrible answer," he said. "I don't know. ... I guess it is a question every man must answer for himself. ... I don't like this war. I don't want my son to be here. I don't want you to be here. Did your friend die for anything? I hope so, if only because there is something in him that lives in you. Every man who dies can live on in us. We can carry him in us and learn from him, and we can answer the question you ask in many different ways and still make his death matter. If you think the answer is no, that this war is wrong, then you can live with his memory and see that this never happens again—that no one dies in another war that is wrong."

There were many other snippets in the book that point out lessons about war. I chose these three as examples for America today. War is an aphrodisiac; human beings choose either flight or fight when confronted with fearful situations. And when the opportunity to flee is gone, every being will fight. Even rabbits, when backed into a corner, where flight is no longer an option, will fight. When you've been afraid to long, and everyone in war is afraid, fighting becomes the seminal instinct. Many if not all soldiers soon learn to love the fighting—a love that is sensual and almost sexual in nature.

Race relations can easily be pushed aside when there are bigger issues to deal with. Would that Americans accept that fact in all instances. We as Americans have bigger issues to deal with, and most have little to do with the color of one's skin. We are Americans first, last and always; let's get beyond the pettiness of race.

And finally, "an answer," not "the answer." Peterson, through his character in the book, suggests that each and every one of us will answer the question about dying in a war differently, based in large part by how we feel about the war—popular or unpopular, supportive or non-supportive. The real issue then becomes personal; do we carry on the memory of those who died or do we work to ensure another war does not occur?

I do not know if the Vietnam War was a just cause worth the lives of 58,000-plus men's and women's lives. I personally have chosen to carry those lives as memories and work to maintain America as the great shining light on the hill of freedom. Others work equally as hard to keep us out of war. To each their own, but surly we all need to understand that in war young people are going to die and our leaders are obligated to justify to Americans, beforehand, the value of war.

Chapter 5
Communion

You've never lived until you've almost died.
For those who fight for it, life has a special
meaning the protected will never know.
——Leigh Wade

In an earlier vignette I mentioned that I may have had my life saved because of a football injury in junior high school. I also felt that injury would keep me out of the Army and therefore keep me out of Vietnam. Wrong. After failing one draft physical because of the knee injury, I ended up passing the second one. But that's another story.

The football injury and my short academic career at Marshall University all came streaming back to me while sitting on top of the Mo Duc (a district town in Quang Ngai Province, Republic of Vietnam) Firebase's tactical operations center, "TOC," the morning after our firebase had been "underrun." I mentioned part of this story in another vignette about Donnie Monn and Biere 33. Sitting there on the TOC in late November 1970 was when I first heard about the plane crash that killed 36 Marshall players and 39 others including coaches and trainers, the plane's crew and team supporters.

Donnie Monn's death, the death of football players, coaches and fans along with the events surrounding the previous night's attack on the firebase was more than I wanted to think about. But it was all there. That's when I heard the helicopter coming in. Nothing really unusual about a resupply bird landing on a firebase, yet for some reason this one sounded much different. Was it the sound of freedom? Don't know.

First to step off the bird was an Army officer, and he was soon followed by four or five cases of beer. The officer turned out to be a chaplain wearing starched jungle fatigues and shined jump boots. You didn't see that too often on a firebase landing zone. Ten or so rumpled Americans made a rush to the beer—go figure. There may be no atheists in a foxhole, but there is no beer either, and we were thirsty for fluid, not God's grace.

Most of us sat there for at least an hour drinking beer, rehashing the preceding evening's events, Donnie's death and Ann-Margret's behind (although none of us had seen her in her '66 tour of Vietnam; Ann-Margret was the American serviceman's sweetheart—at least among the ten of us gathered around a mortar pit that day). That's what tired and scared soldiers do.

Finally, the officer, an Army Captain, came over to where we were gathered and asked if there was anything he could do for us. "Send us home" or "bring on the dancing girls" were the usual replies. However, one of young soldier asked if the Chaplain could serve us "the meal." Most of us thought the soldier was talking about a regular hot meal in lieu of our usual bill of fare, C-rations. But the Chaplin caught on quickly and replied that he hadn't brought his "kit."

No problem, "I've got some water in my canteen and here's a packet of crackers." one of the sergeants said. The rest of us soon caught on—the young soldier wanted the Chaplain to administer Communion, the Eucharist, the last supper of our Lord. So, ten weary, filthy, and somewhat inebriated American soldiers knelt around the sand bags lining a dugout mortar pit and a "strack" Army Chaplain gave us communion using canteen water and crackers.

For me, that communion meant more to me than any other I have received. I know the Lord is with us at all times, but on that day, I felt Jesus' presence right beside me. I felt our Lord free me from fear, and that freedom is profound. The beer that day was the best I have ever tasted, and the elements of the meal the most meaningful. I have never felt so free, and freedom never felt so good!

I don't love war, nor do I believe that being shot at is a good thing; yet, during that tour in Vietnam, full of fear, filth, disgust, sadness, love and loneliness, among the many human emotions, was a time when I felt I was actually doing a job that I was proud to do. I know now what Robert E. Lee meant when he said: "It is well that war is so terrible—we would grow too fond of it!"

John F. Kennedy said, "For those who fight for it, freedom has a flavor the protected will never know." How true!

Chapter 6

Operations Report

When she took her clothes off, I never saw her face.
—Horney G.I.

"War is hell," and General William Tecumseh Sherman intended to make it that way. He was right, war is hell and I'll never belittle the brave men and women who fought in any war. There is nothing funny about war; there's nothing funny about people dying, many in very obscene and unnatural ways. Yet, there is a humorous side to almost every story, even those about or concerning war, and this is one of those humorous stories—at least to me.

To many serving in the field, the Vietnam War took a break most days from twelve noon until 2 p.m. Why? Because it was too damned hot for all combatants, friend or foe. I'll never forget the first time I went into the boonies with a QRF comprised of RF/PF Vietnamese soldiers commanded by my Vietnamese counterpart, the Province G-2. The unit was on a sweep mission looking for a Viet Cong arms cache.

Before I continue, let me define some of the acronyms and nomenclature in the preceding paragraph. A "QRF" is a quick reaction force, usually on standby to react to, in this instance, actionable intelligence. The "G-2" is the chief intelligence officer, in this case in the "province" (like a state) within the country—Vietnam. "RF/PF" are like our National Guard, but on continuous active duty—RF means Regional Forces and PF means Popular Forces. Most Americans referred to the RF/PF units as "ruff puffs." RF/PF units preformed many functions within the South Vietnamese military, such as outpost and guard duties at strategic points, and sometimes as actual combat units like a QRF.

A "counterpart" is an allied (in this case an American) advisor—me. I was a Military Intelligence Officer assigned as the counterpart to the Vietnamese Province G-2. "Actionable" means specific, time sensitive and believable information. A "sweep" operation is exactly what it sounds like—proceed through a designated area, turn over rocks and vegetation, look in huts and sweep up and hold anything that could be used to prosecute war—usually arms, food and sometimes men and women considered to be sympathizers or allied with the enemy.

I was pretty green that day, including the clean green jungle fatigues I was wearing. In fact, I'm sure the Province G-2, Dai Uy (pronounced die we—which is Vietnamese for Captain—I was a Dai Uy also) Kahn, was doing most of the "advising," as he would for at least the following six months. And oh yes, my face was pretty green also, since I was scared shitless—a trait that continued to haunt me for most of my tour of duty in the combat zone.

Don't ever let anyone tell you that they were not scared while in a combat zone—they are either lying or stupid. No one is unafraid when the prospect of dying or being wounded is a possibility. Real soldiers train hard to ensure that muscle memory and mental toughness overcome fear when the shooting starts. There's no "smoke, joke and hang around," like what is portrayed in Hollywood films; there's just fear and reaction when the shit hits the fan. Fear is a great motivator!

So, when Dai Uy Kahn called a halt to our sweep mission at around 1130 hours, established a loose perimeter and hung his hammock between two sturdy trees, I really got scared (even more than I already was). "What the fuck Kahn, what's going on" I stuttered?

"No problem, Dai Uy, VC just as hot as we are, they're taking a nap too. Go over by the river and get a load of the Montagnard (pronounced: "mountain yard" by most Americans) tit show— you like big tits don't you Dai Uy?" was Kahn's retort. Sure enough, I could hear women's voices nearby; we were within a hundred yards of the Ve River.

In a combat crouch, amid much laughing by Kahn and the rest of the unit, I assaulted (really just moved cautiously toward) the riverbank, and lo and behold there were ten or fifteen young women doing their laundry in the river. None wearing any clothing above the waist, and several were wearing nothing at all. Now the Montagnard women were unusually well-endowed when compared to most women in Vietnam in the upper portion of their bodies—yes, they had nice tits.

But beauty ended at the neckline as too many chews of betel nuts (commonly referred to as "beechie nut" by Americans) had turned too many beautiful smiles into lost teeth and a red dyed mouths and gums. Betel nut provided a "buzz" when chewed, but had harmful effects on teeth, gums and the mouth.

Around 1400 hours, the tit show ended and the QRF moved on to the extraction LZ (landing zone) to conclude the day's sweep mission. Our result for eight hours of "sweeping" was 0-0-0-30-5—translated that means: zero arms found, zero food found, zero detainees, 30 nice round boobs and 5 bushes viewed. War is hell!

.

Chapter 7

RIP

*Firm, united let us be, rallying round our liberty,
as a band of brothers joined,
peace and safety we shall find.*

—Joseph Hopkinson

He was a "Full Bird" Colonel, tears in his eyes accepting the applause of those who respected him and were gathered for the reception after his retirement ceremony. Infantry, Distinguished Service Cross, Silver Star, Purple Heart with clusters, Legion of Merit, Distinguished Service Medal, "Master Blaster" Parachute Wings, and Ranger Tab. Colonel Perry had the "full load," so why was he crying?

Fifteen minutes earlier, Chuck, as I was honored to call him, had given a speech that left us all … well, speechless. Quoting Leigh Wade, Chuck had said: "You've never lived until you've almost died. For those who fight for it, life has a special meaning the protected will never know. Friends, I have lived!" And then Colonel Charles Barton Perry (not his real name) went on to relate the horrors of combat in Vietnam.

"I pulled him back from the blast zone of an 82-military mortar—the zone where an incoming round had just exploded and left my friend with a massive gut wound. I held his head with one hand and tried to push his guts back into the wound. All the while I screamed for a medic. Three combat tours in Vietnam, first as a lieutenant, next as a captain and company commander and finally a tour as a battalion commander; friends I have lived."

Chuck was twenty-two years old in 1965 when he deployed with the 173rd Airborne Brigade (Separate); initially he was a platoon leader, and at the very end of his tour he became the company commander for a couple of weeks. Before going home, he was the last officer from the original complement left in his company. The others were killed, wounded or relieved and rotated out.

Three years later he was back as a company commander with the 23rd Infantry Division (Americal) operating in Military Region 1 near Chu Lai, Vietnam. He recalled the turmoil surrounding the Mi Lai Massacre that left a bad scar on the 23rd's reputation. It was during this tour that the events surrounding the wounding and later the death of his friend occurred. Chuck recalled the drug and alcohol abuse by soldiers serving with the Americal Division (quite honestly drug use and alcohol abuse were prevalent throughout Vietnam).

He also recalled the loss of pride by many American troops as the war continued to slog on with little sign of an end. The 1968 Lunar New Year's (Tet '68) offensive by North Vietnamese regular forces and the guerilla forces, referred to most often as Viet Cong, was not particularly an outright victory, yet it seemed to sap the morale of Americans both in country and at home. "The war, after Tet that year, seemed to change," Chuck said. "We were just hanging on instead of trying to win."

Three years later Chuck was back in Vietnam for a third and final tour, this time as a battalion commander. Although just a major (battalions are usually commanded by lieutenant colonels), Chuck was handed the command of a housekeeping battalion (not a combat command) in and around Saigon. Now, off the record, Chuck confided with some of his friends that "this is where the drinking started." A warrior at heart, wiping the noses or kicking the asses of rear-echelon soldiers (referred to as REMF's— short for rear-echelon motherfuckers) was not in Chuck's wheelhouse.

A couple of mediocre efficiency reports and a major who had been destined for the stars, now had to cope with mediocre assignments throughout the rest of the '70s, '80s and early '90s before landing as a colonel in charge of reserves at a CONUS Army base. That's where I met him and was pleased to serve with him on a couple of reserve assignments in 1992 and 93.

Chuck cut the figure of the perfect soldier: tall, handsome, with close cropped hair and a hard body toned by five-mile runs each day. But just as hard as he trained during the day, he drank equally as hard each night. No excuses, but you see, the nights got to Chuck. The nights brought on the nightmares and the demons. Chuck had nightmares about combat (and he had seen plenty in his first two tours in Vietnam) and the demons that came took the shape of poor leaders both military and governmental who ruined the Army that Chuck loved.

In his retirement speech, Chuck lashed out at "political correctness" and policies like affirmative action that, to Chuck's way of thinking, insured that a certain amount of folks would be promoted regardless of their level of competence. "We dumbed-down the Army, particularly the leadership. When we cut the size of the force, we increased the number of generals and senior ranks, like we had to make room for everyone at the top—even those that couldn't lead their way out of a paper bag."

Chuck had more to say that day, and I don't have room to write it down; let me just say, in spite of his demons, Chuck was right, and I'm not sure we've righted the ship yet—just sayin'.

Chuck died the year he retired. Cancer got him, or maybe he just got tired of the "bullshit"—I know lots of us have. Welcome home Chuck, RIP my friend.

Chapter 8
Accomplishment

Mission Accomplished
—A sign above President George W. Bush on a Navy Aircraft
Carrier, somewhere in the Mediterranean Sea.

Many Americans knew exactly what that sign meant, regardless of what the liberal press reported, or regardless of what words the president used. Fighting the war on terror on their soil (the home of the terrorists—the Middle East, e.g., Iraq or Afghanistan) had been accomplished. In retrospect, that mission stayed accomplished throughout the remainder of President George W. Bush's tenure in office. A secondary mission—ridding the world of a truly bad person, Saddam Hussein, was soon to be accomplished as well.

The actor George Peppard starred in a TV series entitled *The A Team*. Often at the end of the show, the George Peppard character would light up a cigar, lean back in a chair, kick up his feet on a table and render the line, "I just love it when a plan comes together." Most plans, and certainly all of the plans envisioned by *The A Team*, fell apart when the team met the enemy. However, *The A Team* had a knack for adapting the plan to fit the situation and bringing the effort to a fitting and usually positive outcome.

Maybe President Bush's plan for the invasion of Iraq, and, continued efforts in Afghanistan, was to accomplish some other mission. Maybe his plan had some underlying political outcome, maybe it was even for his own personal gain, maybe, maybe, maybe. The fact remains that when those plans came together, the outcome was positive. The terrorists (and may God forgive you if you don't know that terrorists are still out there) did not bring the war to our shores, nor did they fight in our streets after the horrific 9/11 World Trade Center incident. I wish the same could be said for W's successor.

And as a "Lucky Strike extra" (the older Americans will remember that phrase), President Bush's initiative rid the world of a very bad man (can you spell Hitler, Pol Pot, Joe Stalin? Saddam Hussein is a name and a person in the same league).

Was the price worth it? Over five thousand Americans were sacrificed to bring about this positive outcome. Americans have mourned and will continue to mourn each and every one of those precious lives—lives given in the name of freedom, liberty and justice. I cannot judge the value, nor can you. I just believe that the world is a better place today without Saddam Hussein, and I know that the terrorists are paying a dear price mostly on their own turf. Mission accomplished, Mr. President, maybe not the planned mission, but a positive outcome paid for at a dear price. Americans understand this.

Chapter 9
1862

The Recent Unpleasantness.
—unknown

I love to write about the American Civil War, so here is another piece, this one relating to events from March through September in 1862.

The Civil War was actually fought in two separate theaters of war, one in the west and one in the east. Most from the Mid-Atlantic area know a lot about the war, as it took place in Pennsylvania, Maryland and Virginia, and they maybe know a little about North and South Carolina's involvement. Yet a thousand miles away from the Union capital in Washington, and nearly a similar distance from the Confederate capital in Richmond, there were numerous battles fought and strategy formulated in states like Kentucky, Tennessee, Mississippi, Alabama, Texas and Georgia. That area is often referred to as the "western theater," or the "trans-Mississippi theater."

The months of April and September of 1862 brought to America arguably two of the bloodiest battles in the history of warfare throughout the entire world. Certainly, the Battle of Antietam (or Sharpsburg if you're of a mind) is clearly the bloodiest one-day battle fought on American soil in our nation's history. That battle was fought about nine miles south of Hagerstown, Maryland—

in the war's eastern theater—on the 17th of September 1862.

In the aftermath of that fateful battle, America's "Little Napoleon," a general hamstrung with "a case of the slows," was sent packing for a second time. President Lincoln received enough of a victory at Antietam Creek to free the slaves "within the States in rebellion," and a Confederate juggernaut was repulsed, ensuring the war would not be over quickly.

In the spring of that same year—April 6 and 7—near a Methodist meeting house called Shiloh Church (the battle commonly bears the church's name), two armies made up of mostly volunteers and generally ill-equipped, met in bungling mortal and bloody combat. The Battle of Shiloh (or Pittsburg Landing), fought using antiquated Napoleonic tactics, cost the Confederacy its "finest soldier" (Albert Sidney Johnston), and sealed the military prowess of a future American president (U.S. Grant).

My short piece will not do justice to the "big picture" surrounding the times, the players, the geography or the Battles of Shiloh and Antietam. So, allow me to recommend two books that paint that big picture in the east and the west surrounding these historically significant Civil War battles.

The first is *September Suspense—Lincoln's Union in Peril,* by Dennis Frye, which is about the Civil War battles of Antietam, South Mountain and Harpers Ferry, and the perilous times facing Abraham Lincoln in the summer of 1862.

You may "take it to the bank," this is Frye at his best. Using newspaper articles and opinion letters from the time, Dennis paints a picture of life as it manifests itself to Lincoln and ties that life into what goes on in the halls of Washington, juxtaposed onto the battlefield terrain. *September Suspense* is good history and a great story. The book is a quick read and will keep readers focused on the politics and the political outcomes during this momentous period in the history of America.

The second is *Shiloh, 1862,* by Winston Groom. Groom is famous for novels like *Forrest Gump* and nonfiction works like *Vicksburg, 1863* and *A Storm in Flanders.* He takes you inside the minds of many Shiloh participants by detailing long-forgotten facts about Confederate and Union leaders, their successes and their failures.

Groom is a master storyteller who blends facts into a seamless period piece that smells of cannon fire, feels of murky swamps and rancid pond water, and captures the horror of the battlefield —all the while, telling about the backroom political deals that seal the fate of soldiers on both sides of the firing line.

It is unimaginable to me to conceive of .58 caliber (that is a barrel size greater than one half inch in diameter) projectiles being fired at distances of less than fifty yards by soldiers standing in opposing lines. Or political leaders sending volunteers to fight without proper food, shelter, equipment, or arms and ammunition; however, such was the case for both sides in 1862.

Frye and Groom do great justice to the stories of the time and will leave you with a true sense of the horrors of Civil War.

Chapter 10
Communications

*The single biggest problem in communication
is the illusion that it has taken place.*
—George Bernard Shaw

In the classroom, teaching for Hagerstown Community College, University System of Maryland, Purdue University (I go back to the days when Purdue, in Hagerstown Maryland, was known as Hagerstown Business College), Mount Saint Mary's University, both undergraduate and master's students, I use a nine-part lecture series on the principles of leadership.

These lectures and the principles they promote are based loosely on lessons learned during the American Civil War. I like to write about some or all of the following principles of leadership: communications, timing, patience, decisiveness, self-assuredness and focus. Remember, these are my opinions about principles that have served me well. You may call them by different names, and some may not appeal to you, while others may have played a role in your own life.

In every aspect of life, and particularly vital in leadership, communication plays a significant role. To my way of thinking, seldom does any positive result occur unless there has been good communication. As far as interpersonal communications are concerned, the basic model (sender to receiver) begins with a thought picture in the mind of the sender. Remember what your mom taught you: "put your mind in gear before you put your mouth in motion!" Just like leadership, good communications always starts with thinking before acting.

Your mouth (verbal) is not the only media for communicating; consider the thought process before writing, gesturing or any other form of communicating. Your mom could have said simply "think before you communicate."

The thinking process is just the first step. Most of us (I really believe it is everyone) filter our thoughts through a process I call "encryption." Each of us has a set of encryption filters that include such things as language, age, race, religion, gender, position in life, income, reality, nationality, perception, prejudices and on and on. Two quick examples of encryption filters: most people "talk down" to children and try to "talk up" to our elders— that's an "age filter." Similarly, most of us talk differently to a "bum" (reality or perception filter) than we do to our "boss" (position filter). This filtering process affects our message and may ultimately effectively limit our ability to communicate well.

What is interesting about the basic communications model is that the reverse of the filtering process occurs on the receiver's side. As a message is passed from the sender, with the sender's thought having been filtered, the receiver filters the message through the receiver's filters—I call this "decryption." A receiver's decryption filters may be the same or different (most often) from the sender's filters.

So, in the model of sender to receiver, we have a sender's thought encrypted, a message passed and decrypted by the receiver, resulting in the receiver having a thought. Here's the bottom line: good communications only occurs when the receiver's thought is exactly the same as the sender's thought; if that does not occur, then only a message has been passed. Great leaders have the ability to communicate, and do not spend a lot of time just passing messages.

During the battle of Antietam, a sender (Robert E. Lee) passed the following message to a receiver (John Bell Hood): "move up alongside hill." Faced with a line of battle to his front that included Generals A.P. Hill and D.H. Hill, as well as a topographical feature that we often refer to as a "hill," Hood was faced with properly decrypting Lee's thought. From Lee's perspective, Hood got it wrong, and heavy Confederate causalities occurred in the now infamous Miller cornfield, as Hood moved up beside the "hill."

Lee was a great leader and Hood likewise, yet, poor communications nearly lost a major battle in the early morning hours of September 17, 1862. Lee, I'm sure, thought he had communicated his intentions, but he merely passed a message.

Chapter 11

Grant

*In every battle there comes a time when both
sides consider themselves beaten, then he who
continues the attack wins.*

—U.S. Grant

Most who know me realize that I am a Southerner, and
generally write Civil War-based articles concerning Confederates
such as Robert E. Lee, "Stonewall" Jackson and Isaac Trimble.
I'm sure some view those folks as a bunch of losers, in spite of
their obvious battlefield leadership traits. So, to be "fair, balanced
and unafraid," this piece is about the ultimate winner—General
U. S. (Unconditional Surrender) Grant. It is fitting that we
remember President Grant during any period commemorating
military leaders and/or U.S. presidents.

I have generally agreed with most historians that Grant was
a "good" military man and a failed president. Recently, due to
discussions with members of one of the book clubs I attend,
coupled with a fair amount of research, I've developed a different
view. I now consider Grant a great military man and strategist,
and an altogether good president, with only certain failings.

First, a few things you may not know. Ulysses Simpson Grant
was not Grant's actual given name. Rather, his name was Hiram
Ulysses Grant. When he registered as a cadet at the United States

Military Academy (West Point) he indicated his full name to be Ulysses S. Grant. Although his mother's maiden name was Simpson, Grant in later interviews about this name change stated that the "S" stood for nothing specific.

At West Point and later in life, Grant, from Ohio, was considered a fine, if not "the finest equestrian ever to sit a horse." This is high praise considering all of the famous horse cavalry officers born in the South.

As a military leader, three personal characteristics are relevant: persistence, offensive-mindedness and relentlessness. These traits pervade any description of Grant. In his own words, "The art of war is simple enough, find out where your enemy is, get at him as soon as you can, strike at him as hard as you can, and keep moving on."

A military man himself, President Theodore Roosevelt noted in a speech given in 1903, "As the generations slip away, as the dust of conflict settles, and as through the clearing air we look back at the mightiest among the mighty dead loom the three great figures of Washington, Lincoln and Grant."

Historian Shelby Foote writes: "Grant the general had many qualities, but he had a thing that's very necessary for a great general. He had what they call 'four o'clock in the morning courage.' You could wake him up at four o'clock in the morning and tell him they had just turned his right flank and he would be as cool as a cucumber ... Grant is wonderful."

Finally, from his old friend, a man who knew him as well as anyone, General William T. Sherman: "It will be a thousand years before Grant's character is fully appreciated. Grant is the greatest soldier of our time, if not all time. He dismisses all possibility of defeat. He believes in himself and in victory."

Similar accolades to those for Grant from Sherman, Foote and Roosevelt were pronounced by others about Gens. Dwight Eisenhower, Colin Powell and Norman Schwarzkopf. Perhaps paraphrasing an old Bum Phillips' quote (Phillips, coach at the time of the Houston Oilers was talking about running back Earl Campbell) might shed some light on where General Grant ranks as a military leader: "I'm not telling you that Ulysses Grant is number one in his class, I'm just saying they're not many in that class."

But great generals have not always made great or even good presidents. Grant is too often remembered for the corruption that occurred during his presidency. Yes, I know that the "buck stops here," and the president is the final buck stopper in any administration. However, no one proved personal involvement in any wrongdoing by President Grant.

On the plus side, and often forgotten, is that the 15th Amendment (the original voting rights amendment) to the U.S. Constitution was ratified during Grant's presidency—certainly one of the most important moves by a U. S. President to secure the freedoms for African-Americans and Native Americans. It wasn't until nearly one hundred years later that a U. S. President (Lyndon Johnson) did anything to further secure the rights of Native and African-Americans. It is amazing how so many historians in the past hundred and forty years have overlooked this important accomplishment of President Grant, which ultimately affected the lives of millions of people.

When remembering presidents and great military leaders, give Ulysses Grant another look. I did, and was pleasantly surprised.

Chapter 12
Grant Versus Lee

If the Union is dissolved and the Government disrupted, I shall return to my native State and share the miseries of my people, and, save in defense, will draw my sword on none.

——Robert E. Lee

During the sesquicentennial commemoration of America's Civil War there was much said and written about the historically great and not-so-great from that time. In this book, I have written about my new perspective on general, later president, U.S. Grant.

A couple of my good friends suggested that I must have had to "bite my tongue" while I wrote about the man who beat my all-time favorite southern hero, Robert E. Lee. The answer to those suggestions was: Yes, at least initially, until I had the chance to really research Grant. However, to be fair and balanced, I guess I needed to do a little more research on my hero, and perhaps that research would result in a new perspective on Lee.

To begin a new look at General Lee my friend Bill Soulis loaned me a wonderful book by Major General J.F.C. Fuller entitled *Grant and Lee, a Study in Personality and Generalship*, 1957, Indiana University Press (the book was originally published in England in 1933). What better way to study Lee than to look at a direct comparison with Grant made by a member of the military establishment?

General Fuller (1878-1966), a British officer, author and historian, is considered by some to be the architect of modern tank warfare. He is the respected author of the nine principles of strategic warfare; those principles, written after World War I, are still valid and used today. I must note that Fuller has his critics, most pointing to his dabbling in the occult, magic and mysticism. But even his critics value his tireless and detailed research.

Fuller concludes: "… Grant is so little understood. Though the greatest general of his age, and one of the greatest strategists of any age, he is little quoted in military histories or textbooks." Grant from Fuller's perspective was the "grand strategist of the Civil War," not the "butcher" and "purveyor of the massed fire frontal assault." Rather, he was a "chess master of maneuver." General Fuller's conclusions are based mostly on his research of the letters, reports, published books and notes from Grant's staff officers.

Fuller uses the same research scheme to frame his conclusions concerning Robert E. Lee. First and foremost, Fuller stylizes Lee as an "aristocrat and a paragon of civility." Lee could bring out the best in others, demanded total loyalty and an absolute sense of integrity. According to Fuller, Robert E. Lee is "the consummate tactical commander." Along with his generals, officers and soldiers, Lee felt that his army was invincible and capable of doing anything under arms.

But as a strategist, Fuller finds Lee lacking. Lee's total focus, after Grant came east, became myopic and was centered on maintaining the sovereignty of his home state—Virginia. Yet the grand strategy for Confederate sovereignty had to include lands beyond Virginia's borders. From Fuller's perspective, Grant was able to grasp the "total war" picture, while Lee was not.

Sharing a similar view with Fuller about "Lee the strategist," Ralph Peters, in his recent book *Cain at Gettysburg*, concludes "At his best, Robert E. Lee fought brilliant battles and admirable campaigns. His weakness was as a strategist: His beloved Virginia was the center of his universe and the need to defend it at all costs blinded him first to the importance of the Mississippi Valley, then to the fatal blows struck by (one of Grant's trusted subordinates) Sherman in the Southern heartlands."

Who am I, but a failed historian, to argue with notable authors like Fuller and Peters about Lee's ability or inability as a strategist? However, in Lee's defense I submit the names of William T. Sherman and George G. Meade, both capable subordinates who carried out the grand strategy of U.S. Grant. With the death of Thomas J. Jackson in 1863, Lee was left with few, if any, subordinates capable of independent tactical action based upon anyone's overall total war strategy.

My overall perspective of Robert E. Lee remains unchanged. If called to go in harm's way under one leader, I would place my sword with Lee.

Chapter 13
Courage

Real courage is when you know you're licked
before you begin, but you begin anyway and
see it through no matter what.
—Harper Lee, *To Kill a Mockingbird*

A good friend of mine called the other day and suggested that I write about courage. Now please understand that my friend was not suggesting that I am personally courageous, rather he knew that I had researched the human characteristic called courage and written about it before.

Courage, a noun, speaks to one's mind or spirit and the ability to "face difficulty." The action most often associated with courage is bravery. One can be courageous in mind and spirit and be, or not be, brave in action. Conversely, an apparent brave action may occur and be based upon other characteristics of the mind or spirit—political expediency comes to mind.

George Washington displayed both courage and personal bravery when he led the vastly depleted American Army, many shoeless, on the Christmas Eve, 1776, sortie across the ice-laden Delaware River to attack Prussian mercenaries fighting for the British.

Newt Gingrich, in several speeches made while running for the presidency, gives a stirring account of this singular moment in

American history. The American army, once boasting 30,000 men at arms overlooking Boston and New York during the summer of 1776, was reduced to approximately 2,500 by Christmas. That year winter came early and was as harsh a winter as most, at that time, could recall. That devastating loss of soldiers brought a compelling reality to Thomas Paine's immortal words about "summer soldiers and sunshine patriots." Truly, those were "the times that try men's souls."

The American Army's password that night was "victory or death." How apropos to the situation; victory would secure the battlefield win that Washington desperately needed. A victory for the Revolution would hopefully fuel continuation of our nation's quest for liberty and independence. Defeat would surely toll the death knell of the army, if not death to its leaders, all deemed traitors by the British Crown.

Later, George Washington displayed a different aspect of courage—moral courage—when he refused a third term as president. This display of courage did not require a requisite show of personal bravery; it was simply the courage to do the right thing.

As is often reported, Washington made that decision because he felt that another term in office might well be considered a return to kingship, prompting the secession of the regular and free elections called for in our Constitution. It was a morally courageous action when you consider that most nations, at the time, viewed bloodlines and divine right as the only way to select leaders.

Through 46 presidents we have had our share of courageous leaders. Madison, arguably our smallest in physical stature, led us to victory in our second war with the British.

Lincoln courageously persevered and preserved the union while freeing the slaves. Lincoln's acts are examples of courage, personal bravery and, more importantly, moral courage.

Franklin Roosevelt, ostensibly an invalid, led us out of the Great Depression, into and out of World War II, and kept our nation focused on freedom. John Kennedy faced down the Soviets over Cuba. Lyndon Johnson brought new meaning to "civil rights" and helped renew our faith in individual freedoms. Ronald Reagan secured victory in the world's Cold War and helped free Eastern Europe from Soviet domination. George W. Bush renewed Americans' faith in our nation's ability to respond to foreign threats in the aftermath of 9/11.

I know my examples of presidents displaying courage may not be agreeable to everyone. Even Washington, Madison and Lincoln had their critics. FDR may have leaned toward socialism. Kennedy must bear some moral questions. Johnson couldn't get us out of an unpopular war. Reagan had his Contras and Bush junior his hurricane and the economy. These are just a few examples of courageous presidents displaying actions that were less than courageous. Not one was perfect, yet in my view each, among others, was morally courageous.

Today, I believe that moral courage—deciding to do what is right in spite of the consequences—among our leaders has been replaced with political expediency and the knee-jerk action of blaming someone else. Too often our presidents, and other national leaders, have passed on taking courageous action in favor of blaming others, or doing only what will help ensure reelection.

I, along with many Americans, wait for another courageous president to emerge. Will it be one with a recognizable name who occupies the seat, or will it be a new face? Regardless, America longs for morally courageous leadership in the White House and in elected offices across our nation.

Chapter 14

Courage Reprise

You will never do anything in this world without courage. It is the greatest quality of the mind next to honor.

—Aristotle

Once again, I'm writing about courage, I have seen many examples of personal courage, as I'm sure you have. In some examples, we may not agree; I say courageous, you say stupid.

Courage is sometimes situational; Indiana Jones ran from snakes, but faced death courageously at the hands of villains. I know a fireman who is scared to death of spiders, yet has no problem running into burning buildings to save lives.

Courage usually has to do with bodily harm or death. Evel Knievel performed "death defying" acts to display his courage. Laying a human life on the line for the entertainment of an audience has been described as courageous from the beginning of time.

I'll never forget the prize fight between Randall "Tex" Cobb and Larry Holmes back in 1982. Some will remember that fight as the night Howard Cosell quit as a commentator at boxing matches. In fact, a battered and bloody Cobb quipped at the end of the fight that in losing he had given a great gift to his sport— Cosell's retirement. More to the point, this fight may well have been the greatest mismatch of all time. Cobb did not win a single round on the card of two of the judges, and had just one winning round on the score card of the third judge.

For fifteen rounds, a total of 45 minutes on the fight clock, Tex Cobb was pummeled by Holmes' fists. Cobb was defenseless to Holmes' attacks; once, in the twelfth round a Cosell associate commented that Holmes would have to stop hitting Cobb because Holmes' hands were hurting so badly. Nonetheless, Cobb's courage in taking that beating has been glorified in fight circles for over thirty years.

I could write for days about acts of courage; some would agree the acts were courageous, while others would see the same act as stupidity. Why would anyone jump the Grand Canyon; why didn't Tex Cobb just stay seated in his corner at the end of the third or sixth round when it was apparent that he couldn't win the fight? On the other hand, should anyone stand by and not try to save another human being from a fiery death? Therein lies the conundrum of courage.

The line between courage and stupidity is surely thin. Is it courageous or stupid to stand up for what is right in your mind, while in another's mind that same "right" is considered "wrong?" Outside of bodily harm or life and death dilemmas, and given a well-thought-out approach, I would suggest that it is always courageous to stand for what in your mind is the "right" action. The outcome of that action may appear to be misguided to some, or the result may become unsatisfactory; however, it is, in my opinion, courageous to stand up for what you believe.

My mother always said, "It's better to do the right thing than to just do things right." Most Americans understand the difference.

Chapter 15
Perspective, WWII and Vietnam

World War II brought the Greatest Generation together.
Vietnam tore the Baby Boomers apart.
—Jim Webb

I'm writing again about Memorial Day and what that day means to Americans. And recently I received a new perspective about the day, as well as war memorials in general. A new good friend, Mr. Al Salter (rest in peace Al), a historian and World War II veteran, commented on my, and Ruth Anne's, radio show: "The World War II Memorial (the one in Washington D.C.) is a memorial to glory … while the Vietnam Memorial is a memorial to grief." Glory and grief, both are heartfelt emotions experienced by those who visit either of these memorial sites.

Al went on to explain: "World War II may be the only war in the history of our country where the vast majority of Americans totally and completely supported the war effort. Once we were in it, everyone got behind it and celebrated the 'glorious' victory. While on the other hand, the Vietnam conflict fractured the American bond; some supported the war efforts and others completely opposed it. The net result, when the conflict finally ended, was a sense of national grief."

To put the World War II memorial in context: "It is here, on the National Mall in Washington, D.C., where the United States 'proudly' proclaims the continuity of our Union and protects the memories of those who have struggled to maintain and perfect it. The World War II Memorial occupies a place of honor along this central vista and takes its rightful place among some of the great icons of American history. The memorial recognizes a period of 'unprecedented national unity' during the defining moment of the twentieth century. Further, through its elements of stone, water, bronze and words, the World War II Memorial strives to honor the service of more than sixteen million men and women in uniform, the contributions of countless millions on the home front, and the unforgettable sacrifice of 405,399 members of our Armed Forces" — a memorial to glory.

On the other hand, "The Wall," or more properly, the "Vietnam Veterans Memorial" reminds us of a war where Americans were divided, a war that ends with no one celebrating a victory. Even the end became a time of grief for many.

Contrasting glory and grief, the World War II Memorial is etched with many great statements spoken by great people, while at The Wall the only things spoken are the names—names carved on a black and somber wall. The World War II Monument is a bright symbol of unity depicting hope and a better future. The Wall is dark, a monument to grief and a reminder of disunity. Such are the contrasts as Americans from "the greatest generation" and from the "counter culture generation" reflect on the horrors, glory and grief of war.

My good friend Chief Warrant Officer 5 (Retired) Fred Shinbur, a Vietnam Veteran, and Maryland's Veteran of the year in 2011, also a guest on the radio show, agrees that the emotions of glory and grief differentiate the two memorials. "I had friends on both sides of the Vietnam War issue. However, I have never met a person, from the time, who believed that the U.S. involvement in World War II was unnecessary or not the right thing to do."

Like other memorials, such as those dedicated to our American Revolution that speak to Tories versus Patriots, or the Civil War—North versus South, or World War I—our president, "kept us out of war" before leading us into it. These memorials portend a victory evolving from disunity. Each of these memorials reminds us that we can revel in the outcome of victory and national unity; even the price in human sacrifice seems to be worth the positive results. Similar to these other memorials, the World War II Memorial elicits many of those same emotions.

Less than one "klick" from the World War II Memorial is the statue of The Three Servicemen and the Vietnam Women's Memorial. The faces on the statues are shrouded with vacant stares, longing perhaps for a glorious victory, national unity and a celebration to thank them for their service. Those statues face The Wall that speaks only to the names of those who paid the ultimate sacrifice.

Yes, Al and Fred, I knew that the three of us, along with veterans of all wars, will reflect on the glory of victory and the freedom it brings. And many of us will ponder the grief that hangs heavy on our hearts—God Bless America.

Section 4

COUNTRY

*This nation will remain the land of the free only
so long as it is the home of the brave.*

*This nation was conceived in liberty and dedicated to the
principle—among others—that honest men may honestly
disagree; that if they all say what they think, a majority of
the people will be able to distinguish truth from error.*

——Elmer Davis

*Freedom is never more than one generation away from
extinction. We didn't pass it to our children in the
bloodstream. It must be fought for, protected and handed on
for them to do the same, or one day we will spend our sunset
years telling our children and our children's children what it
was once like in the United States where men were free.*

——President Ronald Reagan

Our country, the United States of America, is a very
complex organization. What with 50 separate states and even
more territories all having different but similar governmental
structures, geography, laws and even languages, you can fathom
the complexity. Yet the one thing that makes this complex
organization into a county is the simple idea of personal liberty:

"the state of being free within society from oppressive restrictions imposed by authority on one's way of life, behavior or political views."

And you cannot fathom personal liberty without considering the concept of freedom, or being free. So, this section of the book deals with aspects of freedom, liberty and in some instances the restrictions imposed on the people by authorities—some good, some bad.

My purpose is to cause you to think. To think about voting, taxes, laws and the type of leadership you desire from federal, state and local governments. I have my opinions about all of these aspects of a country, and I hope you'll form your own opinions and exercise your right to express those opinions.

And finally, I hope to spur in you a thought about our flag, our Pledge and our Constitution. So, enjoy Section 4–Country.

Chapter 1
9/11

Where were you when the world stopped turning?
——Alan Jackson, singer/song writer

Where were you on a day, or on a date, or at the time of an event? This is a usual question among friends when the subject is the past. Where were you on Kristallnacht, or night of the broken glass? The surviving relatives and friends of European Jews can tell you—they remember the night when the evil that became the Holocaust moved into high gear.

Where were you on December 7, 1941? World War II vets and their families easily answered that question when I visited the World War II monument one Father's Day. My father-in-law, a World War II, Korean War and Vietnam Veteran remembered that day for two reasons: first, it was his 19th birthday, and second it was the beginning of the sacrifice for Americans that was the great world war.

Where were you on 9/11? We don't even need the year to bring on those memories of the day that evil visited our nation. The famous country singer Alan Jackson immortalized that date in my mind and the minds of many Americans, when he called it "the day the world stopped turning."

I was in the studio of local TV station taping a promotional spot for an upcoming United Way campaign. My wife was less than three miles from the Pentagon, in Washington, D.C. A good friend was passing through the quiet countryside of south-central Pennsylvania, on his way to Pittsburgh, when emergency vehicles passed him to reach an already downed airplane. And "let's roll" became etched in our lexicon as a new symbol for fighting tyranny and terrorism.

It has taken a while, but my Christian sense has helped me to forgive those misguided people, funded and urged on by evil terrorist cowards ("forgive them for they know not what they do"), but nothing save for losing my mind or my death will allow me to forget the events of that September day.

If I were king for a day, I'd decree that every American watch, every day, those towers in New York City fall. I'd decree that every day that Americans and our loyal allies go in harm's way to counter the evil threat of terrorism be considered a day of righteousness, not a day of condemnation or second guessing of our national will. My friends, don't ever forget the day the world stopped turning.

There are at least 3,412 stories, from that day, and in reality, more than 250 million stories, as Americans everywhere were affected by the events surrounding 9/11. I'll not tell them all, but I do want to mention in one short vignette, 343 stories from that day.

I have written about this incident before; however, it still bears retelling. The New York City Fire Department is equipped to fight fires in buildings from the outside, up to twenty stories in height. Simply put, the finest fire-engine ladders will only reach up two hundred feet. Fires in buildings over twenty stories must be fought from the inside.

The World Trade Center Towers were over one hundred stories high, and the fires set by the crashing of the planes into the buildings were above the 56th floor in each of the towers. That situation, at first in the North Tower where the first plane entered the building at the 78th floor, confronted over six hundred fire and rescue men and women of the New York Fire and Police Departments.

When the first responders arrived at the North Tower, there were over 16,000 humans still inside both towers. Those first responders arrived before the second plane hit the South Tower. So, imagine standing there or just going into the North Tower and feeling the second plane hit.

Now it's into both towers; can you contemplate climbing through smoked filled stairwells while you hear the sound of elevators crashing to the first floor from as high as the 78th floor, those elevators crashing with living people still inside of them? And then, both towers collapsed.

Among the three thousand-plus deaths that day, 343 New York firefighters gave their lives in one of the greatest displays of sacrifice in the history of our nation.

For those 343 souls, and another 3,100 souls, and for 250 million Americans who have a story about that day, I'll not forget! May you be healed in your heart, may there always be forgiveness, but in your mind never forget the sacrifices made the day the world stopped turning.

Chapter 2
Republic

A republic, if you can keep it.
—Benjamin Franklin

Our U.S. Constitution established the United States of America as a republic. A republic is a state in which supreme power is held by the people and their elected representatives, and which has an elected or nominated president rather than a monarch.

That seventeen-page document, over 200 years old, has a continuing impact on us as citizens, and has had a similar impact on each state's constitution, as well as local governing documents. Therefore, the U.S. Constitution, along with state constitutions, coupled with local government charters, establish the way we are governed.

The Constitution of the United States of America as originally signed in 1787 (and to date has not been changed except by amendments) included a base document consisting of seven articles. Ten amendments were ratified by the states in 1791; beyond those first ten amendments, there have been seventeen additional amendments.

An interesting note of history, what we refer to as the first ten amendments to the Constitution, or the Bill of Rights, are actually the third through the twelfth amendments as initially proposed. Of those originally proposed amendments, one has never been ratified by the states, and proposed amendment number two was ratified in 1992 as the twenty-seventh amendment—marking over 74,000 days in "ratification limbo" since originally proposed.

The Tenth Amendment, or if you will, the last of the Bill of Rights, is probably today the most controversial. That amendment states in simple terms that powers not given to the federal government in the Constitution are reserved to "the States and the People." This amendment has always begged the question, what are the powers of the federal government?

From a layperson's point of view (I certainly qualify as a layperson—I am no lawyer, nor a judge, nor do I profess to understand the nuances of constitutional law—I'm just going to call them as I see them) the federal government, according to the Constitution, has the power to tax you, collect those taxes, pay the federal government's debts, regulate foreign and domestic trade, raise and regulate a military including "militias," declare war, sign treaties, establish a post office, coin money, have a central bank, regulate weights and measures, issue and enforce patents and copyrights, regulate immigration, appoint judges and generally provide for the welfare, as appropriate, of the people.

Although a somewhat lengthy list of powers, the reality is the federal government has fairly limited powers, unless you view providing for the welfare of the people in a broad sense. In that sense—a broad view of providing for the welfare of the people— is what the federal government, specifically the Congress and the executive branch, has done. Do you see a specific provision in the powers listed above (or go online and read the full document for yourself, it is only about seventeen pages long, including the amendments) for federal power over public education, health and human services, energy, housing, etc., etc. I don't!

So, who has those powers? In this short lesson on constitutions, I'll use Maryland's State Constitution as an example. Although each state's constitution is different, Maryland's is pretty standard—not overly restrictive, about average length, has amendments including a bill of rights and serves as a basis for local charters (local governments).

Maryland's constitution, the current one is the fourth in the state's history, ratified in 1867, has a Declaration of Rights which includes forty-seven articles, plus an additional nineteen articles that cover specific state and local powers, e.g., municipalities, the state militia, counties, courts, the City of Baltimore, education, the lottery, public works, the departments of state government, and more. In simple terms the Maryland State Constitution states that if the people of Maryland didn't give it (specific power) to the federal government, then the people of Maryland reserve those powers to themselves! This is correctly stated and in concert with the U.S. Constitution.

The state constitution (Maryland's in this example) speaks to local and state powers not noted in the U.S. Constitution, and further concedes all other powers to the people (in a representative democracy that becomes the basis for laws passed and approved by representative government bodies elected by the people).

So, this begs the simple question: Who do you want to be in charge of your children's education, your health care, your property rights, your retirement, your roads, much of your public safety, the environment, etc., etc.? Should the power over your day-to-day lives reside in Washington, your state capitol, your local government or at the ballot box? I have my own opinion; I think good government is best served closer to the people.

Sure, we need a central government, and states have differing situations that require some form of unique governance, and finally local governments are needed to keep us from anarchy and vigilante law.

Wake up Americans, become involved with government and the exercise of your rights. Any time we centralize governmental powers beyond the parameters established in constitutions and charters, we as citizens lose our precious rights.

Chapter 3
Patriotism

My country has been very good to me;
I must be good to my country.
—Walter Annenberg

My theme and topic in this vignette is patriotism and the love of freedom displayed by our forefathers and more so, the price of that freedom paid by those early patriots. I fear that today, as Americans, we "doth protest too much" about what we are owed. Each day more and more people are not willing to pay a price, any price, for the freedoms and opportunities that we have. Often Americans are more concerned about what is owed them than the price that has to be paid.

Whether it's what the government owes individuals or groups. Or that we are owed compensation when we don't want to work. Or even some argue that everyone is owed equally, regardless of the fact that some give more while others give nothing.

I recently read the third in a series of historical fiction books penned by former Speaker of the House of Representatives Newt Gingrich and William R. Forstchen. This final book in the trilogy, titled *Victory at Yorktown*, recounts General George Washington's audacious actions in the late summer and early fall of 1781 to win our nation's war for independence. Granted, this book is fictional, yet Gingrich and Forstchen are well known for presenting historical facts in the back and foregrounds of their work.

We all know the outcome of Washington's, and a rag tag army of patriots' actions—we won our independence from the British Crown. However, many of us have lost sight of the price those patriots paid. Also, often lost to history, are the friends that helped make that independence possible.

In Gingrich's and Forstchen's dedication of the book they remind us of "our all but forgotten allies, the French troops and sailors who insured our victory at Yorktown. In a world where, at times, friendships of old can be forgotten, we should always honor the memory of the aid France gave us in our struggle for liberty, and in turn, the sacrifice we offered back in the great struggles for freedom in the twentieth century."

Since the Revolutionary War, in all contests on the global stage, the French have been our friends. France gave much, as our friend, for our freedom and did not collect what we owed them for over one hundred years.

Forgotten also are the civilian friends of the Revolution, some never having worn a uniform—friends, such as Robert Morris. In the concluding three months leading up to the Battle of Yorktown, Morris mortgaged his personal fortune twice to pay the Continental soldiers (those same soldiers had not been paid for many months in coin or script that had any real value).

Upon realizing that he had pledged one hundred percent of his personal assets as collateral for an earlier debt to pay for military supplies and equipment, before he pledged them a second time, Morris mused "they can only throw me in debtors' prison once." Like every signer of the Declaration of Independence, Morris had staked his life and sacred honor upon the cause of freedom. Morris and many other civilians literally gave much, were owed much, and collected little in return for financing a war to preserve our present-day opportunities.

And lastly, Washington and his army all gave some, and some gave all. That's not trite; tens of thousands were killed, wounded or just went missing. At the same time, all gave some—officers and private soldiers alike prosecuted a war for our freedom with little (if any) pay, meager rations, no shoes or suitable clothing and limited or nonexistent shelter. Yet they stood in firing lines, manned artillery, and rode horses into battle to defeat the greatest military power (at that time) in the world—giving us today the freedoms and opportunities we often times take for granted. In the end, few collected anywhere near what they were owed.

Our nation is founded on a premise that through freedom, all have opportunities. Our freedom has been bought and paid for because some gave all. However, today only some pay for all of our opportunities, while others just feel they are owed. As an American, pray for those who gave all, and those who give some. But pray harder that, one day, all will give some.

Chapter 4
Voting

*I hold it that a little rebellion now and then is
a good thing, and as necessary in the political
world as storms in the physical.*

——Thomas Jefferson

I can't help it; I have to comment on the recent primary and
general elections. No, this is not a statement about who won and
who lost, although, in my opinion, there were a couple of scary
names on the winner's side of the results. Nor is this a statement
about how campaigns were conducted. Rather, it's about our
rights as Americans, how to protect those rights and how to
participate in self-government.

Oh, silly me, I forgot, there are plenty of really good reasons not
to vote: "I was out of town." "I didn't know it was Election Day."
"My work doesn't allow me time off to vote." "I was sick, tired,
or not feeling well." "I didn't know anyone who was running."
"There were too many running." "It's just the same old crowd."
"My vote really doesn't count," or "my one vote doesn't mean
anything or won't make a difference." Or my very favorite, given
to me recently: "I gave up voting for Lent.". The excuses for not
voting go on and on and on.

Absentee voting, early voting, extended voting hours, voter
aides, elimination of the poll tax, no voting examination or tests,

touch screen voting machines, large print voting screens, increased voting locations, handicap accessibility to voting places, motor/voter registration—all of these innovations and changes to voting procedures render all excuses for not voting moot.

If you are alive, and want to vote in most states you can and it is generally very easy. (I expect that in some states you don't even have to be alive.) So, the real "reason," for not voting boils down to the fact that many don't "want" to vote. To me that is sad commentary.

I have written many times that in my opinion the greatest "right" that we as Americans have is the right to vote for those people who represent us and govern our lives. This is what Jefferson speaks of when he praises rebellion.

But is your right to vote cemented in the Constitution? The Constitution contains many phrases, clauses and amendments detailing ways people cannot be "denied" the right to vote. However, the Constitution does not expressly guarantee Americans the "right to vote."

For instance, you cannot deny the right to vote because of race or gender. Citizens of Washington, D.C. can vote for president; 18-year-olds can vote; you can vote even if you fail to pay a poll tax. Note that in all of this, the Constitution never explicitly assures the right to vote, as it does the right to free speech, for example.

Aside from these requirements concerning who can vote, the specific qualifications for voters are generally left to the states. As long as a state's qualifications do not conflict with anything in the Constitution, only the state may withhold the right to vote.

For example, in Texas persons declared mentally incompetent and felons currently in prison or on probation are denied the right to vote. The 26th Amendment requires that 18-year-olds must be able to vote, yet states can allow persons younger than 18 to vote in certain elections.

Although I'm not a constitutional lawyer, I contend that my right to vote is equally assured to me along with my right to free speech, religion, possession of arms, protection from unlawful search and seizure, et al, as outlined in the Constitution's Bill of Rights. I cannot fathom the possibility of a government, national, state or local, denying a qualified American the right to vote. Hell could not contain the fury!

So, vote (just like the Cook County, Illinois, Democratic "machine" used to recommend—early and often)! Seriously, participate in government; choose who makes the laws and decisions that affect you. You do that when you vote. Exercising your right to vote is truly the American way. Be faithful to Thomas Jefferson and join the rebellion each and every time you are allowed to vote.

Chapter 5
The Flag

Standing as I do with my hand upon this staff,
and under the folds of the American Flag, I ask
you to stand by me as long as I stand by it.
—Abraham Lincoln

The following vignette I wrote several years ago; however, with all of the furor in recent years about standing, kneeling, saluting and being disrespectful to our flag and anthem, I believe the words and sentiments are still timely.

I wrote earlier about our nation's "Pledge of Allegiance" to our flag. Not to be boastful, I received several kind and supportive comments about the prose. Some asked for my reference sources, and I'll freely admit most of the information in the vignette came from simply Googling the Pledge on the internet. Personally, I usually look at two or three different reference sources to ensure the information contained is essentially the same before I rework the information into my style.

I was pleased that others found the information contained in that piece interesting and informative. I too learned some new "stuff" while doing that simple research. Sadly, in my opinion, today we don't know as much as what our forefathers knew, particularly in the civics, history and geography arenas, and sadder still, I fear our children are learning less in those areas than we know.

No judgment here, but it seems to me that younger folks today find playing "Modern Warfare 33" much more interesting than reading James McPherson's historical account of the battle of Gettysburg. Go figure. I still have faith that there is a silver lining out there somewhere; however, enough of the soapbox rhetoric.

I attended an event recently, and while talking to one of my friends hc noted that the American flag was not displayed properly. Before my friend could rectify the situation, the program started. Afterward, I decided a piece about American flag etiquette and protocol might be in order. Here are some rules concerning our flag, taken from a section of federal law generally referred to as the "Flag Code."

The American flag should be lighted at all times, either by sunlight or by an appropriate light source and should be flown in fair weather, unless the flag is designed for inclement weather. The flag should never be dipped to any person or thing. It is flown upside down only as a distress signal. The flag should not be used as part of a costume or athletic uniform, except that a flag patch may be used on the uniform of military personnel, fireman, policeman and members of patriotic organizations. The flag should never have any mark, insignia, letter, word, number, figure or drawing of any kind placed on it, or attached to it.

When the flag is lowered, no part of it should touch the ground or any other object; it should be received by waiting hands and arms. To store the flag, it should be folded neatly and ceremoniously. When a flag is so worn, it is no longer fit to serve as a symbol of our country, it should be destroyed by burning in a dignified manner.

When the American flag is displayed or carried (e.g., in a parade or procession) three general rules apply: In a static display on a pole. the American flag is always displayed in the prominent position (forward of other flags, in a center position) or on the flag's right (your left if you are facing the flag). When carried, the flag is always forward of other flags or if in a line of flags on the flag's right. When displayed on a horizontal halyard or other attachment the flag's union (the blue portion with the stars) should be up and to the flag's right.

Okay, now that you know some of the rules about our flag, do you know what color of red, white and blue should be used? The official specification for federal procurements of U.S. flags is set by the General Services Administration. At the Defense Technology Information Center is GSA "Federal Specification, Flag, National, United States of America and Flag, Union Jack." It specifies the colors by reference to "Standard Color Cards of America." This is a color system designed for textile use, which is appropriate, since flags are made of cloth! The specifications are: No. 70180 Old Glory Red; No. 70001 White; No. 70075 Old Glory Blue.

Ever see an American flag with a gold fringe? That's the Army's and Air Force's version of the National Colors. Both services use this version of the flag for display with other organizational colors and in parades. The seaborn services do not use the gold fringe. Rather, their versions of the National Colors are displayed with red, white and blue cord and tassels. I wonder what the new Space Force will do relative to their version of the National Colors.

I could go on for pages, but I'll suggest you do your own research and gain a greater sense of love and respect for our flag.

Chapter 6
The Pledge

The Pledge of Allegiance reflects the truth that faith in God has played a significant role in America since the days of the founding of our country.

—Randy Neugebauer

I spoke several years ago on a cold February afternoon, at a Presidents' Day luncheon in a local church on the subject of patriotism. After beginning the talk with vignettes about several of our forty-five presidents, my remarks turned to our Pledge of Allegiance, then to the flag. What is more patriotic than reciting the Pledge, hand over heart, facing the Stars and Stripes of this great nation?

As Americans, our way of life has, for over 200 years, been based upon liberty and justice for all. Patriots, both men and women, have lived and died serving beneath our national flag—the symbol of our liberty and justice—defending and protecting our way of life. Pausing to reflect on those sacrifices, the simple pledge to our flag is a small price to pay for the many blessings of liberty and justice we have accrued as Americans.

The Pledge of Allegiance was written in 1892 by Francis Bellamy, a Baptist minister. The original Pledge of Allegiance was published in a September 1892 issue of a popular children's magazine as part of the national public school celebration of the four-hundredth anniversary of Christopher Columbus' arrival in the Americas.

Bellamy's original Pledge reads as follows: "I pledge allegiance to my flag and the Republic for which it stands, one nation indivisible, with liberty and justice for all." That original pledge has been modified three times. First, in 1923, the National Flag Conference called for the words "my flag" to be changed to "the flag of the United States," so that new immigrants would not confuse loyalties between their birth countries and the United States. Second, the words "of America" were added a year later.

The United States Congress officially recognized the Pledge for the first time in the following form, on June 22, 1942: "I pledge allegiance to the flag of the United States of America, and to the republic for which it stands, one nation indivisible, with liberty and justice for all."

The final change, adding the words "under God," was a bit more convoluted. Louis Bowman was the first to initiate the addition of "under God" to the Pledge and was awarded a medal by the Daughters of the American Revolution for, in their opinion, being the originator of the idea.

At a meeting on February 12, 1948, (a Lincoln's birthday celebration), Bowman led the society in swearing the Pledge with the two words, "under God," added. His rationale was that the words came from Lincoln's Gettysburg Address. Though not all manuscript versions of the Gettysburg Address contain the words under God, all the reporters' transcripts of the speech do. Lincoln may have deviated from his prepared text and inserted the phrase when he said "that the nation shall, under God, have a new birth of freedom." Later, the Catholic Church's Knights of Columbus began using the words "under God" in the Pledge each time it was rendered.

Several times, during the period from 1948 until February 1954, attempts were made to have the words "under God" added to the Pledge through an act of Congress. Those attempts failed.

The final successful push began with George Docherty. Docherty, the pastor of Washington, D.C.'s, New York Avenue Presbyterian Church preached a sermon on February 7, 1954, with President Dwight Eisenhower in attendance. The sermon was based upon Lincoln's Gettysburg Address.

In his sermon, titled "A New Birth of Freedom," Docherty opined that the United States' "might" lies not in its arms, but rather in "its spirit and its higher purpose." He noted that the Pledge's sentiments could be those of any nation, that "there was something missing in the Pledge, and that which was missing was the characteristic and definitive factor in the American way of life." He cited Lincoln's words, "under God," as defining words that set the United States apart from other nations.

Eisenhower had recently been baptized a Presbyterian, a year before. He responded enthusiastically to Docherty in a conversation following the service. Acting on Docherty's suggestion, the next day, February 8, 1954, Rep. Charles Oakman introduced a bill to that effect. Congress passed the necessary legislation and Eisenhower signed the bill into law on Flag Day, June 14, 1954. Eisenhower stated, "In this way we are reaffirming the transcendence of religious faith in America's heritage and future; in this way we shall constantly strengthen those spiritual weapons, which forever will be our country's most powerful resource, in peace or in war."

Presidents and a Pledge, good partners on a cold February afternoon; thank you Presidents Lincoln and Eisenhower!

Chapter 7
United

The Destiny of Man is to unite, not to divide. If you keep on dividing you end up as a collection of monkeys throwing nuts at each other out of separate trees."
—T.H. White

On Saturday, July 7, 2007, I saw something I thought I would never see. A liberal Democratic governor from a blue state read the words of Abraham Lincoln, arguably a founder of the current Republican Party, to a crowd largely comprised of conservative red staters. Upon completion of his reading, Governor Martin O'Malley (governor of the State of Maryland, at the time), received a standing ovation. Wonders have never ceased to amaze.

I had to hand it to Governor O'Malley, his reading at the Maryland Symphony Orchestra's presentation of Aaron Copland's *Lincoln Portrait* was excellent. So was his speech earlier in the day to a gathering of folks celebrating the groundbreaking of a solar energy project at the state prisons.

O'Malley's first words at the solar celebration were about jobs. And jobs, in Maryland and all across the nation, were important. His second comment was how glad he was to see folks with differing political views sitting together in celebration and not in an ideological debate.

Oh, the boo-birds said that the jobs O'Malley spoke of were "government provided" jobs, or the jobs were just employment for those who already had a job. But to someone without a job, you don't care where the job came from. My friend "Dutch" Ruppersberger, Congressman from Maryland's 2nd Congressional District at the time, told me once that "the greatest social program in America is a job." I doubt Dutch originated that statement, but whoever did coin it made a lot of sense.

Other boo-birds then said that O'Malley's comments about celebration and not debate was just a poor attempt at humor. However, given the place and time, along with what took place later, I felt Martin O'Malley was being sincere. You see, the MSO concert was held at the Antietam Battlefield Park

My purpose in this story is not to make a political statement. I'm not asking you to vote for O'Malley (he ran for President in 2016) and I'm not endorsing him for any office. Yet, for just a moment, it was refreshing to put politics aside and hear a man I would disagree with on many issues speaking about something good for our community, our state, the environment and this great nation.

When I lived in Maryland, my home was in a conservative area in arguably the most liberal state in America. Yet I have not heard anyone voice an attack on America or our freedoms—no one, not liberals or conservatives, Republicans, Democrats, Independents, Green's or Tea's. Just like it was in the 1860's our politics often divide us, but freedom and liberty unite us.

There were 24,464 American casualties on one day in one battle at Sharpsburg, Maryland along the Antietam Creek. Sure, some came from the South and others from the North, but all were Americans. All fought for freedom that day, yet certainly both sides viewed individual and national freedom in differing ways.

On that battlefield, September 17, 1862, some were Northerners, some abolitionists, slave owners, Southerners, staterighter's, unionists and on and on. Yet all were Americans fighting for freedom and liberty as each perceived those inalienable rights. Sadly, on that day and on other days at venues across this nation it took a civil war, where many died, to settle the differing perceptions.

But on the same Antietam Battlefield, during that MSO concert, folks with differing political views sat together, heard stirring words and stood in applause when Governor O'Malley read from several of President Abraham Lincoln's most eloquent words. Would that we all could sit together, hear stirring speeches, find common ground for all of our differences and stand united as the great nation that we are.

Ratchet forward to the present time and pray that we can settle our political difference in a peaceful manner. The ballot box is the battlefield for revolution!

Chapter 8
Leadership

*Sometimes by losing a battle you find
a new way to win the war.*
—Donald Trump

I've written about leadership from my own personal point of view several times in this book. I've discussed several guiding principles that I believe make great leaders, including communications, patience, decisiveness, and timing. This vignette is about self-assurance and focus.

A good friend of mine, a local politico elected to public office several times, offered to me a great strategy to ensure an elected body focused on doing good for the folks that elected them. I'll not mention my friend's name, or the elected body; let's just leave it as someone local, not anyone on the state or national scene.

At the beginning of each year in the term, the elected body would meet in a retreat or closed session. During that meeting, each member of the body would be asked to name a number one project, program or issue. The only caveat was that the project, program or issue must be capable of coming to fruition or completion within the forthcoming fiscal year. After debate among the body and the consideration of input from staff, citizens, or stakeholders, as well as some negotiation and tradeoffs, the individual selections became the top priorities for the body for the coming year.

When the top priorities were set, individual members of the body had to agree to the list and resolve to not criticize, backbite or vote against any of the top priorities. Of course, this resolution was not binding and certainly situations surrounding money, law and constituents' pushback often altered the priorities. The point, however, is that this strategy created focus on a group of priorities that were, at least in the corporate mind of the elected body, good for those who elected them.

Dose that strategy always work? Of course not, yet this is an example of a leader creating the focus for those who are led. There is only one thing my friend left out of his strategy; the ultimate focus must be on outcomes, not just completing the project, program or issue.

Case in point: General Ulysses S. Grant, as commander of all Union armies in 1864, realized that winning individual battles (similar to successful completion of a project, program or issue) was not an overall winning strategy. The ultimate and necessary outcome for the Union was to win the war.

Each time Confederate General Robert E. Lee thwarted Grant's efforts to win an individual battle—the Wilderness, Spotsylvania Courthouse, Cold Harbor, et. al.—Grant simply moved around Lee and remained focused on winning the war.

Another case in point: The successful commanders (leaders) of Roman armies often placed their least powerful legion in the middle of the battle space. This invited the opposing army to attack the middle, focused on overwhelming that portion of the line. As this occurred, the center of the Roman line would retreat, allowing the Roman flanks to entrap the opposition. Opposing armies attacking the Romans often focused on the wrong thing— the weakness in the Roman line—and missed focusing on the ultimate and necessary outcome—winning the battle. From a leader's perspective, focus is an important principle, as long as the leader is focused on the right thing.

Finally, self-assurance is often referred to as being cocky or arrogant, mostly by those that don't have it. Seldom do great leaders succeed by accident. If you don't believe in yourself, generally others don't. Human nature dictates that most folks will not follow a pseudo-leader who starts out to finish second. Finishing second is first loser. I could go on and on, but you get the point.

Doak Walker, the famous running back for the Detroit Lions, noted that quarterback Bobby Layne, the leader of the team in the 1950's "never lost a football game, he just ran out of time; nobody hated to lose more than Bobby Layne." Bobby Layne, the leader of the team, displayed self-assurance; give him the ball and you had the opportunity to win—regardless of the score.

U.S. Grant, with his back to the Tennessee River at Pittsburg Landing on the night of April 6, 1862, called his depleted staff and his division commanders together and predicted, "we'll win this thing tomorrow." That's self-assurance. Grant's army had been thoroughly routed by Major General Albert Sidney Johnston's Confederate Army of Mississippi on the first day of the Battle of Shiloh.

However, on day two of the battle, the self-assured Grant, communicating well with his subordinates, applied a patient, well-timed, focused and decisive counterattack that turned defeat into victory. This is leadership personified.

Chapter 9
Government

Government's first duty is to protect the people,
not run their lives.
—Ronald Reagan

And while the law of competition may be sometimes hard
for the individual, it is best for the race, because it ensures
the survival of the fittest in every department.
—Andrew Carnegie

Why do liberals distrust business and love government, or why do conservatives distrust government and love business? Well, neither "why question" is reasonable because neither is true in all cases. However, if you listen to the political rhetoric going around today you might think both statements are true in all cases.

Case-in-point, many liberals espouse a larger government model with less reliance on business for economic development. Is this liberal love of one and hate for the other? Maybe it is more a case of trust in one and disdain for the other—and God only knows that businesses have committed their share of disdainful acts lately. On the other hand, our trusted government is supporting or partially supporting nearly half of our nation's population—that trust is fine until the credit runs out.

Another case-in-point, many conservatives want a smaller government model with more reliance on business to move the economy forward. As a conservative myself (not a "presumptuous liberal elitist" as some would have you believe), I personally disdain bigger government with its move to control every aspect of my life. I still trust the business model and see that model, in a free market, as the best opportunity for economic growth. Many of my conservative, as well as liberal, friends agree.

Beyond the issue of economic development, I could make many cases in point—but I'll avoid specific comparisons and write about the functions each government and business do well. Now, before you fire up the comments, I wrote "do well," not "do perfectly," and I'm talking in general terms, as I'm sure you or I can point out specific instances where neither government nor business has performed well.

I'll take government first. Government holds (you could say owns), maintains and improves property very well. I'm talking buildings and/or lands—look at the National Parks or government buildings within the District of Columbia for specific examples of the federal government's noteworthy efforts in the property-holding arena. Locally, states and local governments also generally do good work maintaining school houses, libraries, public safety facilities and park facilities.

National defense (or public safety, if you want to carry the function of protecting our citizens to the state and local levels), is clearly in the government's "do well" column. Although I'm sure some of my good friends believe that the National Rifle Association could do it better if we'd just approve eight-inch howitzers for private ownership—just kidding. I believe most will agree that our defense and public safety are in good hands with our governments. Of course, there are other functions, many others, that government does well.

On the business side, the best words to describe "do well" abilities will usually speak to competition and efficiency.

Durable goods production is best kept with the business sector where competition usually keeps prices lower. Simply put, the efficiencies competition brings to production generally mean lower prices and technological advancement—both good for almost everyone. Research and development are also better served in a business model, where premiums reward success for doing things better, quicker or less expensively.

I could go on and on about either side in a comparison of functions done well by business or government—it would just make exhaustive lists and fodder for arguments, and not prove anything except that both entities have their place in the world as we know it.

All of that comparison aside, I heard an economist on National Public Radio contend that the organization and structure of democratic government as we know it through history after the monarchy period is the same or a similar model to the business corporate organizational structure.

Governments have their voters, corporations their stockholders. Governments have legislatures, corporations have boards of directors. Governments have executives (presidents), corporations have CEOs. Governments have constitutions, corporations, charters. Governments have employees, corporations, workers. And finally, both serve citizens or consumers or humankind, whatever you want to call you and me.

For all practical purposes, government and business, particularly those businesses organized as corporations, are similar, and operate in a similar manner. Both perform some functions well and others not so well—yet both are necessary.

Neither government nor business can be everything to everyone. Both have their places in our world; we cannot live in freedom and prosperity without one and the other. Therefore, any arguments should revolve around where functions are performed well and not about which model is best.

Chapter 10
Cooperation

What works in the real world is cooperation.
—William J. Clinton

Here's a story about cooperation between political parties, community leaders, lobbyists and the business community. In the national scene this is a small-scale project, yet the cooperation displayed should be a model for projects regardless of the scale.

In July of 2009, the governor of the State of Maryland signed the Fiscal Year 2010 Capital Budget Bill; somewhere on some obscure page was a line item for the expansion of the Western Maryland Regional Library, and that line totaled five million dollars in state money for 2010, with a guarantee of another five million dollars in Fiscal Year 2011. What is ironic is that a couple of weeks before the end of the legislative session, that line wasn't in the governor's capital budget at all. How did that line get into the final bill? Well, let me tell you. It got there through the cooperative hard work of the Western Maryland community.

Oh, Delegate John Donoghue (a Democrat in the Democrat-controlled House of Delegates) and Senator Don Munson (a Republican in the Democrat-controlled State Senate) worked the system to actually get an amendment to the budget bill in the pipeline, and then kept it in during debate in both the House and Senate of the General Assembly. For those efforts each, Donoghue and Munson, deserve special thanks. But the story doesn't start or end with those efforts. There's more, much more to the story. Our local delegation (heavily Republican) stood together in support of the library expansion, voted in favor of the amendment and ultimately the capital budget bill.

High ranking Democrats in the Maryland House and Senate worked hand in hand with local Democrats and Republicans to ensure that Maryland state funds were allocated to the library expansion project. Why would Democrats support a heavily Republican delegation (Washington County) on what was easily perceived as a local Washington County project? Because it is the right thing (not the parochial thing) to do for the citizens of our community and Western Maryland.

Put your personal political views aside for a moment and celebrate the fact that the "D's" and "R's" can work together. Statewide or even national agendas should not get in the way of doing the right thing.

But wait, there's more! Even locally, those sometimes-quarreling governments, the city and the county, got together in total support of this project. In fact, the City of Hagerstown, a government with no mission responsibility to support public libraries, put up $1.5 million to support the overall library expansion project. Our local governments can and do work together. When our governments, state and local, work together the citizenry will benefit.

How about lobbyists? Yes, we paid some and they also helped get this library project funded by putting local community leaders in front of decision makers within the state. Those lobbyists are the first-line defense when other entities attempt to move against the best interests of our community. Celebrate the fact that our community recognized the need for lobbying service and put together a coalition of governments and private sector groups to move our community into the state arena as players, not just "those people" from Western Maryland.

It certainly didn't hurt to have our own "National Librarian of the Year," Mary Baykan, and her staff working hard with state representatives and state library officials to bolster support for our library project. Celebrate the fact that our local library system, home of the first bookmobile, is recognized nationally as one of the best of 3,800 library systems in the nation. The Board of Trustees (of which I was proud to be a member) supported Mary's efforts, working hard to make this project a cooperative effort among state, county, city and even the federal government.

And finally, celebrate the role of the much maligned "business community" (you know the people that bring jobs to the community); yes, they also had a role in this library project. The business community helped fund our community lobbying effort, plus many members of the business community spent countless hours in Annapolis working to put the pieces of a project strategy together that manifested itself in this major library expansion. Some say that Maryland is not business friendly, but our local business community continues to put the community's wellbeing and continued prosperity as a top most goal in spite of a sometimes business unfriendly atmosphere. Our local business leaders know that when the community succeeds, business will succeed.

I know I've been a bit "Pollyanna" in this prose, also a bit lengthy, and probably stepped on some toes. I also know that the picture I have painted of this very successful government/business/community effort will have to bear the "warts on the pickle" that will ultimately appear. Opinion authors will ultimately point out any flaws in the project, or the fact that the project didn't appear in some master plan, or who knows what else. But celebrate with the citizens of this community that we do have a positive community self-esteem, that we do, as a community, deserve good things and that when we work together, and stand together, governments, businesses, and citizens alike we can achieve great things for our community.

This story demonstrates the power of cooperation, which is what most Americans want today. My good friend Tim Rowland stated in an opinion piece that eighty percent of Americans are in the middle, centrists, moderates or whatever label appeals to you. The other twenty percent are on the right and left extremes. Simply put, most Americans believe in cooperation—when the principle of cooperation is applied the sky is the limit on what can be achieve.

Chapter 11
Taxes

We have a system that increasingly taxes
work and subsidizes nonwork.
—Milton Friedman

Let's talk taxes. My mom (and Ben Franklin) told me that the only two things that are certain are death and taxes.

Many politicians nationwide have signed pledges to "not raise taxes" or to levy "no new taxes." I bet some even wanted to say "read my lips," and we all know how that worked out back in 1988. Heck, I voted for the guy; then Vice President George H.W. Bush used that phrase at the National Republican Convention in his acceptance speech as the Republican standard bearer for president. That year he won.

Four years later, after President Bush did implement new taxes (or at least raised some existing ones), an upstart Democrat from Arkansas used those infamous words to block a Bush second term. Strong political statement: "read my lips, no new taxes"— very tough to make good on such a promise.

I remember my second-grade teacher, a large lady (my mom called her "stout") yelling at me: "If you don't sit down and shut up, I'm going to throw you out of that window." Scary. Twenty years later I went back to that second-grade classroom and looked at the window. It was about 36 inches by 48 inches in total size, but was covered then, as it was twenty years earlier, by a steel grill work with only 4-inch square openings in the grill. Not even the smallest seven-year-old (and boy I wasn't one of them) would fit through those squares. Like "read my lips" my teacher's "…throw you out that window" pledge was a strong disciplinary statement, but one she could never make good. However, to a second grader it sounded totally plausible.

Such is the way with much of the political rhetoric surrounding tax pledges—sounds great, what the people want to hear (or don't want hear about), but virtually impossible to carry out. Particularly if you're in the minority party, leading on issues such as taxes is a daunting task at best.

I've said it several times, it's worth saying again: "I don't want my taxes raised any more than you do"; "I am not an advocate for higher or more taxes." I am, I like to believe, a practical person and I believe, just like my mother told me, that taxes (raised, restructured, lowered, expanded or whatnot) are inevitable.

What I do want is for all of us to quit the "blame game"— whether it was those vile and evil Democrats or those upstanding, truth, justice and the American Way Republicans (really, my tongue is in my cheek) who got us into this economic mess, it really doesn't matter. Getting out of the mess does, and idle and hollow pledges are not the answer. Taxes on the other hand, new or old, are inevitably going to be part of any solution.

I believe that what most of us want—at least when we think about it at a level higher than a second grader—is tax reform, or tax restructuring, or maybe just tax simplicity and equality. Regressive tax, progressive tax, flat-rate tax, need tax, use tax—I'll let the smart folks explain all of that stuff; it's far too complicated for me to explain in a short vignette.

However, from my simple perspective, if elected officials want to pledge something to me about taxes, then here is my list: 1. Pledge to simplify all tax codes, no exemptions, no loopholes;

that spells equality. 2. Pledge that every eligible taxpayer, no exclusions, pays some taxes—no one gets a free ride. 3. Pledge that whoever pays a tax receives some benefit for the payment, and that the taxing authority be required to continually explain the benefit in simple terms.

If those same elected folks want to be really creative and capture my attention completely, then they should pledge to work "across the aisle" with all other elected folks to determine what government does with the taxes. Sure, what I have outlined is virtually impossible to implement in its entirety, so in some ways I am just as guilty as the "political pledgers." But some of it can.

For many of us today, taxes, particularly higher or new ones, feel like being thrown out of a window might feel to a second grader: scary. So, elected officials, scare us with some fresh ideas on revamping taxes and justifying how tax money is spent. And finally, scare us to death by actually working together, not blaming each other. That's the American way!

Chapter 12
Taxes Reprise

The only difference between death and taxes is that death doesn't get worse every time Congress meets.

—Will Rogers

Frequently I talk or write about taxes and what I believe are "tax pledges" that would capture Americans' attention. So, as outlined in the previous chapter, here are some examples. 1. Simplify the tax code, no exceptions, no loopholes. 2, All eligible taxpayers pay the taxes, no free rides, equal to all. 3 Everyone who pays the tax receives a benefit from the tax and further, the taxing authority must continually explain the benefit to taxpayers in terms of specific use and accountability.

Now, I'm going to pick a tax as an example. I am not proposing the following as a new tax; I am only using this as an example, although timely, that would be true to my proposed pledges. For my example I choose increasing the national fuel tax by ten cents per gallon. Most folks I have talked to believe that our federal, state and local roads are deteriorating and may soon become unsafe.

Pledge one: Increase the current tax by ten cents for every gallon of petroleum-based fuel dispensed. The revenue from this tax will be used to build and maintain roads. The tax will be collected by the federal government.

Sorry, anyone who today gets a break on petroleum-based fuels: its ten cents a gallon if it has petroleum in it (whole or part, so no exemptions for the ethanol additives, or any other additives). Simplicity.

Pledge two: Every user (taxpayer) pays the tax, so no exemptions for governments or anyone else. Every ten cents per gallon goes into a tax revenue fund for roads. Equality.

Pledge three is maybe the easiest. On every "dispensing unit" for petroleum products, there would be an easy-to-read sticker that says "ten cents per gallon of the cost of this product goes to a fund that provides roads for this nation"—or something like that. If you, as a voter and a taxpayer, ever get the notion that some government level is not spending that tax revenue on roads, then vote the person or persons out of office. Specific use and accountability.

Now, what do you do with the revenue? The feds collected it, so give them a tenth of a cent per gallon dispensed to administer the program. Here's where it gets interesting. Any idea how much a tenth of a cent per gallon of gas dispensed in America equals?

In Fiscal Year 2006, according to the federal government, Americans used 378 million gallons of gasoline per day, equating to nearly 138 billion gallons of gas used just for personal and commercial cars and trucks (this does not include fuel for airlines, the governments, farms, industry, et. al.). A ten cent per-gallon tax on just this fuel usage alone would equate to 13.8 billion dollars in tax revenue, and with a tenth of a cent allocated to administration, the federal government could set up an agency with a budget of approximately 140 million dollars (I'm pretty free with tax dollars. but this is just an example).

Now, take half of the remaining 13.6 billion dollars and dedicate that to federal roads (the Interstate system, for example). Again, for illustrative purposes, if Interstate highways cost an average of one million dollars per mile to build (that is probably an old cost but I believe you'll get my drift), then this nation could build a totally new Interstate system every six-and-one-half years (there are approximately 46 thousand miles of Interstate roads in the U.S. today).

In my simplified model, give the other 6.8 billion dollars to the states and local jurisdictions for use on state and local roads. I'm sure there is a simple formula that could fairly allocate those funds based on gas sales or road miles, for example.

Far too simple, sure, yet my thesis remains: taxes, fees, tolls or whatever name we call the government's revenue stream is inevitable. Americans deserve to get what they pay for; if we want good, safe roads then there is a cost. In my example that cost is a tax imposed on gas usage. It's simple and equal, with a specific and know benefit for the tax.

Legislators have more important work to do than to make idle pledges about "no new taxes." At all levels of government, legislators need to work on multi-partisan efforts to ensure accountability and wise use of public money; that's the American way.

Chapter 13
Olympics

On these fields of friendly strife are sown the
seeds that on other fields, and other days,
will bear the fruits of victory.
—General Douglas MacArthur

Even though two winter and two summer Olympic Games have concluded since I wrote the following piece, I firmly believe the national sentiment surrounding the 2012 games is America personified.

On the thirteenth of August, 2012, I asked myself the question that I'm sure was on many an Olympic junkie's mind: now, what am I going to watch on T.V. for the next four years? Yes, I'm an Olympic junkie, yes, I bleed red, white and blue; yes, I always root for the Americans.

Don't tell me about the person from country X or Y, how that person worked hard, ran from war, and had a disability or whatever, and that I should root for them. No, on the field of athletic competition I root unashamedly for the American Olympians.

Yes, some of our Olympians are jerks and egocentric, poor winners and losers, yet during the competition I root for them all. In spite of their character flaws, or their open mouths with feet inserted sometimes past the ankle bone, these Olympians still represent our country—and I am proud of these athletes and proud myself to be an American.

Other than serving our country in desperate situations or in harms' way, representing our country on the fields of athletic competition is a rare honor only afforded to a few. I'll always cheer for the Americans' effort even if an individual athlete's character or the example they set is flawed.

Speaking of athletic competition, did you know that during modern era Olympic Games, "tug of war" has been an event. Seems that tug of war was ultimately scrapped because matches took as long as seven hours to conclude. It would be tough to show a long match live during prime time—sure would take up a lot of "up-close and personal" segments.

Premodern-era games included Olympians competing nude; that sure makes the skimpy beach volleyball outfits a little more palatable to even the most prudish viewer. By the way, the least stressful match to watch in the entire 2012 Games, at least for me, was the gold medal women's beach volleyball final. U.S.A. versus U.S.A., gold medal assured, I relaxed and enjoyed the view.

Weren't our swimmers wonderful, new blood, old blood; pass the torch; youth will be served; veteran experience; and any other athletic cliché you may wish to use. However, you describe the competitors and the American program, it looks like our swimmers will continue to dominate into the future.

In track and field, aren't those Jamaicans fast? It kills my soul that Americans are no longer the world's fastest, but just like the long-suffering Chicago Cubs fans, in my house it's "wait till next time." Also hurting American pride was losing the 4x400 relay for the first time since the 1972 games. What looked like poor baton passing in the finals and a broken leg in a prelim negated some of our usual speed edge in that event.

Our women's soccer (that's football for you blokes from the Euro-zone, and other parts of the world) and water polo teams were just awesome. Tough preliminary matches toughened our ladies, and I'm sure helped firm up their resolve in the gold medal round. Not just from me, but from lots of junkies, direct to our women's soccer team: "Don't leave us hanging for so long, coming from behind three times in one game is nearly heart stopping—way to go ladies!"

Once again in the "subjective sports"—you know, the ones that allow judges to award scores—the Americans came up a little short. So, tell me, what does the splash have to do with the diving score, or the dismount with the gymnastic routine?

Our shooters made all of us Second Amendment folks proud by taking early honors in several rifle and shotgun events. Putting the guns aside, how about those basketball shooters? Men, women, dream team, greatest team ever—it's our game, we invented it and we're the best at playing it, enough said.

Even in my zeal to support the U.S.A. team, I was disappointed with our modern pentathletes. The pentathlon has always been the "soldiers' sport"—running, shooting, fencing, swimming and horseback riding. Our best in the Olympic event this year was 32nd place. Maybe we ought to teach some Navy Seals or Army Special Forces soldiers how to ride and fence.

All told, there's really nothing to be disappointed in, most total medals—U.S.A.; most gold medals—U.S.A. No boycotts, no political statements made on the podium and no terrorist attacks, just athletic completion among the nations of the world. Those games were an Olympic junkie's dream come true.

Now it's on to Rio, Japan and beyond. U.S.A., U.S.A., U.S.A.!!!

Chapter 14
Environment

What's the use of a fine house if you haven't got a tolerable planet to put it on?
—Henry David Thoreau

Two of my friends asked me, after reading some of my work comparing business with government in terms of structure, to comment on corporations (business) relative to the environment. So, here's my take!

First, let me say that there are no absolutes. Nothing I say in favor of a business model relating to the environment or opposing business as it relates to the environment is "always" true or correct. That leads me to opine: "generally" business is not the enemy of the environment, nor is the environment "always" protected by business. Much the same is true for government. Finally, the environment may not need all the protection that business or government attempts, or is required to provide.

Speaking of a need for protection, many may point at crude oil spills in the oceans. "See, business is wrecking the environment, killing fish, water fowl and all sorts of ocean-going creatures!" Well, yes, oil spills in the oceans do that, but it is not the intent of business, or even Big Oil to create oil spills. In simple terms, no oil company I know of goes out of its way to spill oil into the oceans of the world—period! Oil spills, from an "intent" point of view, fall in the category of "doo doo happens," regardless of the number of rules, regulations, laws, agencies and such that are in place to protect the environment.

Therefore, my next opinion about business vis-a-vis the environment is this: "generally" business or the business model does not intend to spoil or harm the environment. As always, you the reader may find some examples of gross neglect or even outright efforts by business to circumvent rules, laws and regulations where the result of those actions does in fact spoil the environment. However, I suspect that no one can relate a willful trend to ruin the environment across the broad spectrum of business.

Case in point concerning neglect or possibly even intent, in the 1980's Union Carbide built a chemical plant in Bhopal, India, allegedly to circumvent United States occupational health and safety regulations. India, at that time, was not as strict concerning environmental, health or safety standards as was the United States. Nor did India have a similar set of rules, regulations and laws. The net result of that overseas operation allegedly was the untimely death of thousands of Indians due to unsafe working conditions at the Union Carbide plant.

Further, the chemical spill associated with the deaths allegedly ruined a portion of the environment in India. I always hate to use the word "allegedly," however some businesses, some government agencies and some individuals take great umbrage with opinions stated as facts without the backup of "legal proof." Therefore, in this example, I'll settle for alleged and let you research the proof.

That leads me to my third statement about business and the environment: Many times, business is hamstrung by overzealous inspectors and monitors of the law, rules and regulations, as well as overzealous law makers making laws that often defy a common-sense test. Businesses are in business to make a profit, while living in harmony with the environment. Laws, rules and regulations should address a business and environmental harmony, and not upset that balance while passing a common-sense test when implemented.

Case in point, lawmakers who have never set foot on a farm sometimes make laws without input from farmers (yes that has occurred, and not just in the farming business). Sure, there are lots of public hearings, public input and lobbying, however some legislation gets enacted based solely on political ideology without apparent thought given to common sense. Then, tragically, during the execution of laws, rules and regulations another layer—the inspectors, monitors and administrators—often add their own non-commonsensical interpretation to the mix.

I've often wondered if the biblical Noah was an environmentalist or a businessman when he worked for God. Did Noah, the businessman, decide, based on an economic development study and a detailed business plan, there was no room on the ark for unicorns (and that's why you've never seen a unicorn to this very day). Or, did Noah, the environmentalist, decide that mosquitoes were an endangered species and loaded up two of those pests anyway? Well, I don't know. But like I have noted previously about business and government, both being necessary, we must never necessarily discount our environmental responsibilities.

Chapter 15
Do the Right Thing

Right or wrong, the customer is always right
——Marshall Field

Recently my brother-in-law spoke at a Rotary Club meeting; his topic was "Business Policy is Personal." Although I did not hear his presentation, I asked Dan Duncan to loan me a copy of his talking points so that I might incorporate some of his thoughts in this book.

His opening for the presentation went something like this: "Business policy is personal because policy affects many people at many levels within and outside the organization—for example, leaders, managers, employees, customers, partners, competitors and such."

In this vignette I'll broaden the concept of policy to include rules and procedures, not laws. Laws in this context are rigid; policy, rules and procedures speak to some degree of flexibility. It is this flexibility that I want to write about.

Also let me broaden the scope of policy to include government policy as well as business policy. All citizens of a governmental jurisdiction are customers of that government, just like the users or buyers of goods and/or services are customers of a business. A long way to come to a thesis statement for this piece: "Government and business policy affects customer service on a personal basis."

Let me use a couple of instances to illustrate how policy can be personal when it comes to customer service. A couple of years ago I went to a local golf course to play with my regular group. That day I wore a shirt with no visible collar. The golf pro approached me and said that it was the course's policy to not allow golfers to play in shirts without a collar. As the pro approached me the first thing I noticed, even before he said one word, was that he was carrying three extra-large golf shirts with collars. After he explained the course policy, he went on to ask me to pick one of the shirts in his hand, pointed me to the locker room to change and then said, "have a great round."

Last year, I traveled to a course about an hour and a half south of my home to play. I wore shorts that were made of denim material. Once again, a golf course employee approached me and said, "You can't play here in those shorts, it's against our policy." turned and walked away with not even a suggestion about how to mitigate my situation. I guess you can figure out where I play golf today.

I am not naive enough to think that all policy, rule or procedure disputes can be solved as easily as handing over a "loaner shirt" to someone who is attempting to operate outside the policy's limits. However, I am practical enough to know that many policy, rule and procedure disputes can be settled with a little emphasis on customer service.

Sure, I know that the department store chain known as Marshall Field's has gone out of business and has been acquired by Macy's, but the founder's famous quote, "right or wrong, the customer is always right," remains a foundation block for good customer service everywhere. Field went on to say: "Goodwill is the one and only asset that competition cannot under sell or destroy."

Good customer service and goodwill, both ideals focus on a positive attitude, flexibility and a vision to succeed. Both ideals must be staples in business, as well as government, if either is to be successful.

In government, just like business, success is "how can we do that," while failure is "we can't do that." In Dan's summation to his presentation on policy and personal, he presented a card issued by a previous Commanding General of the U.S. Army Corps of Engineers. The card was given to all of the Corps employees. The card reads: "Permission Slip. Ask yourself: 1) is it good for my customer; 2) is it legal and ethical; 3) is it something I am willing to be accountable for? If so, don't ask permission; you already have it. Just do it!"

Loaner golf shirts, on the spot waivers of bureaucratic technicalities, paying it forward and assuming some risks are just a few examples of business and government building goodwill and practicing good customer service. Like successful businesses, our government, at every level, needs to remember that you can't oversell goodwill or have too much good customer service. Good customer service in business and by our government is good for America!

Chapter 16
Rebellion

*Disgusting, cowardly creatures, the ambivalent. Worse than
the fallen, in many ways.
They have no conviction at all.*
— Cynthia Hand, *Boundless*

From the book *Winter of the World* by Ken Follett, speaking
of the ambivalence and apathy of many pre and post WWII
Germans, Follett writes, "… those inadequate people who were
so scared by life that they preferred to live under harsh authority,
to be told what to do and what to think by a government that
allowed no dissent. They were foolish and dangerous, but there
were an awful lot of them."

To compare Nazi Germany and Communist-controlled East
Germany with America today is not altogether farfetched; certainly,
our government is not "harsh" in terms of the enforcement of
laws. However, if you equate the number of laws, regulations
and rules created by a continuously growing government at the
national and state levels to a degree of "harshness," then Follett's
assessment of pre- and post-war Germany is closer to being a
parallel assessment of our current situation here in America.

Further, although we as Americans continue to have many
ways to dissent, would we be prone to disagree if dissent or
disagreement was tied directly to our living conditions and

wellbeing? Case-in-point: If the government paid for your health care, your food, your shelter, your transportation and generally subsidized to a greater and greater extent your total wellbeing, would you disagree (dissent) with your government's actions? How about your government's actions in other areas such as foreign affairs, public safety, business, development, growth?

Sure, some would (disagree or dissent), but others would not. Many people ascribe to the old adage of "not biting the hand that feeds you." And when we stop biting the government's hand, what will happen to our republic?

I find the following information ironic: James McHenry was an early Maryland statesman. McHenry was a signer of the United States Constitution and the namesake of Fort McHenry. In his diary, McHenry recorded this conversation: "Outside Independence Hall when the Constitutional Convention of 1787 ended, Mrs. Powel of Philadelphia asked Benjamin Franklin, 'Well, Doctor, what have we got, a republic or a monarchy?' With no hesitation whatsoever, Franklin responded, 'A republic, if you can keep it.'"

McHenry, the story goes, was moved by Franklin's assertion about the future of our republic and if we could keep it. A republic, as you know, is simply a representative democracy. Would we be able to elect those who would uphold the values noted in the fledgling Constitution? Would our future as a nation include electing leaders that would uphold our rights and liberties and ensure that government itself would not become as tyrannical as those governments headed by monarchs or dictators?

After a typical Maryland General Assembly ninety-day session, where over 2,500 bills (possible laws) are processed, I cannot help but wonder how a latter day "Maryland statesman" would respond to an inquiry from a citizen about whether our state government today is more like a monarchy (where the government is totally in charge) or a republic (where the people through their elected representatives are in charge)? And if you think the Maryland state government's control continues to grow, how about the federal government, how about other states and localities?

Consider: "America was founded by men who understood that the threat of domestic tyranny is as great as any threat from abroad. If we want to be worthy of their legacy, we must resist the rush toward ever-increasing state control of our society. Otherwise, our own government will become a greater threat to our freedoms than any foreign terrorist." —Ron Paul, *Texas Straight Talk*, May 31, 2004

As a conservative Republican, it pains me to quote a "tea party" ultra-right winger, yet words are words and what is spoken, if it makes sense, are words to the wise. Paul may be right. Ken Follett in his fictitious work about Nazism, Communism and Fascism in the 1930's and '40's, coupled with Paul's words sends a chilling message of watchfulness to those of us living today.

When we depend on government—too much—we position ourselves for failure and give up our right to independence and self-governance. Thomas Jefferson reminded us over 200 years ago to always be in a state of rebellion. Each year that there is an election, that is your day to rebel. Rebel at the ballot box; vote for those who will represent you by supporting less government and will protect your individual freedoms. And every time there is an election, join the rebellion again!

Chapter 17
Environment Reprise

*Listen up, you couch potatoes: each recycled
beer can saves enough electricity to run a
television for three hours.*
—Denis Hayes

Before you read further, answer for yourself; do you believe that recycling is a good endeavor? Now don't put in "economical" or "cost effective," forget the price tag. Also, don't "Al Gore" yourself by considering your position on the environment, our children's future, global warming or the continued existence of three-eyed tree frogs (I just can't help a small jab at the guy who invented the internet). A simple yes or no answer please.

If you answered no, then read no further because I expect you are already angry with local governments that support or require recycling. Also, I've probably heard from you, or one of your personal representatives, at the local convenience store where you were smoking a cigarette, drinking a 32-ounce coffee (five creams and six packs of sugar) and poking me in the chest and telling me how stupid government is (the cigarette and coffee part is all true, but you were really just poking my ears with uninformed drivel).

Back to "read no further." Immediately after you finished your last drag on your "ciggy" (your word, not mine), you flicked said ciggy into the parking lot and barely missed the store lady who was sweeping up all your friends' ciggys from earlier bombastic pontifications about the stupidity of recycling, war and peace, the price of pork belly futures, or the national debt. Heck, I bet you even emptied out your truck's ashtray before you left the parking lot, because there were just too many ciggys on the street at the stop light where you emptied it yesterday. So, if this is you, please, read no further.

If you've missed it, I've begun to equate recycling with "litter." Why? Because I remember the nation's "war on litter" begun in the early sixties. Headed up by Lady Bird Johnson (you remember her: "plant a scrub or a bush today and help our nation stay clean"—or something like that), children, teenagers and young adults were brainwashed on almost a daily basis about the evils of litter.

My dad was a smoker—two, three packs a day, Kool Regulars, unfiltered and laden with menthol (I was sure that he chose that brand to ensure his kids would never filch a pack and take up the habit). He could roll down the side window on our '62 Dodge Coronet (no electric windows in our cars), flick the nub of that Kool out the window, roll up the window and continuously navigate the curvy section of West Virginia Route 13 on the way to our home on "Tunnel Hill."

When he'd go for the nub, my brother and I, in perfect stereo, would relate the latest Lady Bird Johnson speech on litter (this was really tough on Dad as he was the only registered Republican in our county—well, maybe there were a few others). Short story, it worked, the war on litter spawned a generation or two of litter hating Americans. America was cleaned up.

Remember, if you are a "no" answerer, read no further. The biggest gripe I hear regularly, other than the fact that recycling may cause cancer in laboratory rats—just kidding—is that it "ain't free no more" or "those containers are ugly," or the "recyclers just take the stuff to the dump anyway and the government is making money on the taxpayers."

Well, my tongue is clearly in my cheek, and if you've read this far, please allow me to summarize the realities of recycling. First, recycling has never been free, and never will be completely free. Even if you use the "free recycling service" (and there are some provided by local not-for-profits), you will still have the cost of getting the recycling to the collection point. Recycling has and will continue to have a cost. However, if you answered yes to my initial question, you will continue to pay that cost because recycling, like eliminating litter, is a good endeavor.

Second, the recycling containers may be ugly, but the future cost of the clean-up of landfills may make the beauty issue a moot point—power lines are not beautiful, but I bet you're not willing to take them down and give up electricity.

And finally, no one, including the government, is making money on recycling. If they were, a lot of officials would be driving Lamborghinis. Recycling is simply a good thing for all Americans to do!

Chapter 18
Difference

What difference, at this point, does it make?
——Hillary Clinton

I am worried about our nation, and specifically, about our president's welfare. First let me say I did not vote for Mr. Biden in the 2020 election. Mr. Biden and I have many differences associated with politics and ideology. All that said, the president is the president, commander in chief and arguably the leader of the free world, regardless of who holds the office. He is "the man" (or she is the woman if that is the case).

Several times in my past, I have personally sworn allegiance to our Constitution and those leaders appointed over me. The president of the United States is the top leader reflected in that oath, and unless the President violates our Constitution, I have always sworn to defend or protect our president and his office. Regardless of any difference I may have with our president, I would gladly take and execute that oath again today—'nuf said about "differences" and "allegiance."

On September 11, 2012, a group of Libyan, Arab or Islamic terrorists symbolically assassinated our president when they actually murdered his ambassador, Minister Plenipotentiary J. Christopher Stevens. Yes, this was a case of "symbolic assassination" on a symbolic date, and actual murder that may have taken place on American soil.

Let me explain: first symbolic assassination. The Concise Encyclopedia, online, makes the following statement about the concept of Ambassadors: the "highest-ranking diplomatic representative of one government to another or to an international organization. As formally defined and recognized at the Congress of Vienna (1815), ambassadors were originally regarded as personal representatives of their country's chief executive rather than of the whole country, and their rank entitled them to meet personally with the head of state of the host country."

"Since 1945, all nations have been recognized as equals, and ambassadors or their equivalents are sent to all countries with which diplomatic relations are maintained. Before the development of modern communications, ambassadors were entrusted with extensive powers; they have since been reduced to spokespeople for their foreign offices."

Notwithstanding the reduced powers, when on foreign soil, meeting face-to-face with a duly appointed ambassador is symbolically the same as meeting face-to-face with the head of state of the country that appointed the ambassador. Those terrorists symbolically assassinated our head of state when they murdered his ambassador. Don't make it complex, it is just this simple: can't reach "the man," then murder the next best and nearest thing—his ambassador.

Symbolic date: By murdering J. Christopher Stevens on the eleventh anniversary of what most terrorists believe to be the date of their greatest victory over the forces of evil—the United States of America—those terrorists sent a strong statement, at least from my perspective. A statement we should not ignore or call "a bump in the road."

Is the number eleven symbolic? Before I write more let me declare: 1. I'm not an alarmist; 2. I'm not an expert on symbolism, Arab culture or all that is going on in the Middle East; and 3) I am merely a writer with thirty years of military intelligence experience.

Yes, there may be symbolism to the number eleven: "If ten marks the perfection of divine order, then the number eleven is an addition to it, subversive of and undoing that order. If twelve is the number which marks the perfection of divine government, then 11 falls short of it. So that whether we regard 11 (as in 11th anniversary) as being 10 + 1, or 12 - 1, it is the number which marks disorder, disorganization, imperfection, and disintegration.

Could those terrorists have been telling us about disorder, disorganization and disintegration of our nation? Well, I don't know. I just hope our government knows and protects our president. Given the adventures in South America by our Secret Service, coupled with several intrusions into the White House and its grounds, maybe a little fore warning is in order.

And finally, just plain murder on our own soil—the grounds of any nation's embassy or consulate is that nation's sovereign territory. Although the "crime scene" may now be tainted and spoiled, most reports indicated that our ambassador was murdered on American Consulate grounds, and therefore sovereign U.S. soil.

Assassination and murder, whether symbolic or actual, calls for a quick and lethal response. As a nation we cannot allow terrorists to become emboldened by symbolic actions leading to new attacks within our borders. The war on terror is not over and calling a terrorist act an "out of control mob" will not end it. Americans want justice; that's the "difference it makes"!

Chapter 19
Doozy

——A national political campaign is better than the best circus ever heard of, with a mass baptism and a couple of hangings thrown in.

—H. L. Mencken

Well, it looks like we had ourselves a race—the 2020 presidential election—this race looked like a doozy. Now there's a word we don't hear too often—doozy—know what it means?

From Yahoo's Answers comes a reasonable explanation: "Etymologists are fairly sure that it (doozy) comes from the flower named daisy. ... (daisy) was once English slang, from the eighteenth century on, for something that was particularly appealing or excellent. It moved into North American English in the early nineteenth century and turns up, for example, in Thomas Chandler Haliburton's *The Clockmaker of 1836*: 'I raised a four year old colt once, half blood, a perfect picture of a horse, and a genuine clipper, could gallop like the wind; a real daisy, a perfect doll, had an eye like a weasel, and nostrils like Commodore Rodgers's speakin' trumpet." (is that great prose, or not?) "Experts think that that sense—which was still around at the end of the nineteenth century — might have been (further) influenced by the name of the famous Italian actress Eleonora Duse, who first appeared in New York in 1893. Something

227

'Dusey' was clearly excellent ... and it is very likely that it and 'daisy' became amalgamated ... to create a new term"—doozy.

The online Urban Dictionary points at pretty flowers and excellent automobiles: "Something extraordinary or bizarre. Etymology: perhaps alteration of daisy, and Duesenberg, a luxury car of the '20s/'30s. It's an English expression" later Americanized.

Well, if the 2020 presidential election was a doozy, I wonder who'll ultimately be the "huckleberry." So, what's a huckleberry?

Huckleberry is 19th century slang which was popularized, once again, by the 1993 movie *Tombstone*. The term may mean: "I'm the man you're looking for." Today it's usually used as a response to a threat or challenge, as it was in the movie.

In the movie, Val Kilmer, as Doc Holliday, says to Johnny Ringo, "I'm your Huckleberry, that's just my game." Did the real Doc Holliday say this? Well, the first time this quote shows up in print is in Walter Noble Burns' book *Tombstone* in 1928. Burns interviewed many old-timers in Cochise County and may have gotten the quote from one of them. We do know that the saying is Southern and basically means, "If you want a fight, I'm your man." Some believe it has a more devious insult implied, as in, "If you want to dance, I'll dance with you."

The etymology of the phrase may be traced back to Arthurian lore. Huckleberry Garlands were said to be given to Knights of the Kingdom for coming to the service of a damsel. They would approach the lady, lower their lance, and receive the small branch as a symbol of gratitude, much like a medal. Therefore, "I'm your huckleberry" may mean "I'm your hero." But Doc Holliday was no hero in the eyes of Johnny Ringo, and if what I've read in a couple of plant-life periodicals is true, the huckleberry doesn't grow in England.

Other reviewers of the movie believe Kilmer didn't say "I'm your huckleberry," he said "I'm your *hucklebearer*." His accent in the movie makes it hard to hear. In the 1800's little handles on a coffin were called "huckles," an English term. Instead of pallbearers, the people who carried the coffin were called "hucklebearers." Using this definition, maybe why Johnny Ringo got so bent out of shape when Doc said, "I'm your hucklebearer." Doc was telling Ringo, "I'm your pallbearer," or literally, "I'm going to carry you to your funeral." This is maybe why it was so offensive and the shooting started.

Who knows? I like the, "I'm your man" definition. So who, former President Trump or President Biden will get to ultimately call himself the hucklebearer for the other in this doozy of an election? Even though the election is officially over, the friction between Trump and Biden continues—so, hope there's no gunfire this time around.

Chapter 20
Leadership Reprise

*All of the great leaders have had one characteristic in
common: it was the willingness to confront unequivocally
the major anxiety of their people in their time.
This, and not much else, is the essence of leadership.*

— John Kenneth Galbraith

I've written many times about leadership and my opinions
about the important principles that make a good leader. I
explored communications as one guiding principle, and now I'll
write about timing, patience and decisiveness.

Great leadership is often a result of the moment. A great leader
may spend hours in planning an effort or a specific outcome,
only to have the effort or outcome go wrong because of bad
timing. Sun Tzu, the famous ancient Chinese military general, in
his book *The Art of War* states clearly: "Every plan is a good plan
until you meet the enemy." Simplified, every plan that is well
thought out has its time—or, because of bad timing any plan can
go awry. Time can be the enemy.

Take Stonewall Jackson's end run at Chancellorsville; the
timing was both perfect and imperfect during the same event.
Catching Major General O.O. Howard's flank "in the air,"
while Howard's men were preparing supper, was the perfect
time for an attack. Starting the attack with only two hours of

sunlight remaining in the day—a not so perfect time—may have contributed to Jackson's untimely death, and allowed the Union Army to regroup and conduct a somewhat orderly retreat the following day.

While leading my students through leadership studies, I often relate that an A paper late is an F, and a C paper on time can be an A. Just ask any contractor about timeliness in relation to the bidding process. Also, "if you're five minutes early you're ten minutes late" is an old adage that relates to everyone. I remember a simple scenario where my watch and the airline's watch were not in sync—I missed the plane even though I thought I was early.

Union Major General Lew Wallace learned a great lesson about timeliness at the battle of Shiloh during the American Civil War. The lesson learned was "how to lose a battle" … nearly. Wallace, later to become a renowned author with his novel "Ben Hur" took the right road that ultimately became the wrong road and never arrived on the battlefield during the first day of battle. On that first day, the Confederates nearly drove the Union Army into the Tennessee River. Had Wallace arrived on time in the right place, might the ultimate Union victory have been sealed earlier?

Although not attributable to Confederate Major General Nathan Bedford Forrest in any form or fashion, the military adage of getting to the battlespace first with an overwhelming force (often paraphrased as "firstest with the mostest") is truly a reflection of timing and decisiveness. In my mind's eye I see Confederate Major General Ambrose Powell Hill, clad in his red battle shirt, leading his "foot cavalry" division into the exposed flank of Union General Ambrose Burnside's Corps at the very moment when Burnside was aligning his troops to roll up the balance of the Confederate Army at the Battle of Antietam.

I can't be sure it happened exactly that way, however a decisive blow at the perfect time saved Lee's army that day. Luck or leadership, or maybe a little of both, involving timing and decisiveness usually puts the odds in favor of the ones prepared to assume the advantage. If you could, ask Napoleon about the Prussians at Waterloo.

Finally, for this vignette, consider patience as it relates to leadership. Most failed historians (like me) will immediately point at the Revolutionary War Battle of Bunker Hill and Colonel William Prescott's or General Israel Putnam's (most likely no one really said it) famous quote: "Don't shoot until you see the whites of their eyes" as an example of patience by leaders in battle. And who could argue; patience is defined as "calmness under duress," and those farmers and shopkeepers aligned along the crest of Bunker Hill (it really was Breed's Hill) displayed calmness while waiting for an experienced British Army to come into range.

General Norman Schwarzkopf was patient as he quietly deployed an unstoppable force on the right flank of the Iraqi Army during that war. The political pressure to win a quick victory was enormous; but Schwarzkopf knew that patiently deploying an overwhelming force would limit casualties and save American service member's lives.

Whether on the battlefield or in the board room, or even in the home, great leaders are patient and consider timing as an integral part of the decision-making process. And when the decision is made and the time is right, great leaders act decisively to assure success.

Epilogue

I apologize for some of the chapters in this book being a bit dated; also, several examples I use to make points are about West Virginia, Maryland or Texas. However, those are the three states where I lived while writing this book.

I have made an effort to construct not a continuing story, but a compendium of short vignettes about Americans. This is, in my mind, the "One Minute Manager" for some, not all, Americans about life in these United States. I hope it brings entertainment and some value to any and all who read the book. In retrospect this book is about remembrance and freedom—particularly about the freedom we, as Americans, should share.

To close, and to bring you, the reader, up to date, the following are words from a speech I delivered in Richmond, Texas, on 31 May 2021, to a group of American veterans, their families and friends. I believe the words express my true feelings about being an AMERICAN.

Memorial Day 2021

Some of you may have read many of the words I'll speak today in several published articles. I'll be the first to understand if you fall asleep from boredom in the first few minutes, but I hope you will be awake for the conclusion.

As is my usual, let me talk for a few moments about three things: history, remembrance and freedom. First a little history.

Memorial Day marks the unofficial start of summer, conjuring, images of picnics, barbecues or just a lazy day off. But originally the holiday was charged with deeper meaning — and with controversy.

The exact origins of Memorial Day are disputed, with at least five towns claiming to have given birth to the holiday sometime near the end of the Civil War.

In addition to Charleston, South Carolina, Waterloo, New York, Washington, D.C., and Columbus, Mississippi, and a small town in Western Maryland, specifically Sharpsburg, Maryland, which is situated along the Antietam Creek. Sharpsburg always gets my vote as the first town to celebrate Decorations Day— known, of course today, as Memorial Day.

If you are a Southerner, you call the bloodiest day in American military history the Battle of Sharpsburg; if you are a Northerner, you call that same fight the Battle of Antietam.

On Friday, 31 May, 1867, approximately four-and-one-half years after that battle, at high noon, a group of townspeople held a parade to honor the soldiers (both Northern and Southern) who died in that battle. That first parade began near the headquarters of General Robert E. Lee (during the battle), went straight through the main street of Sharpsburg and ended at the newly opened Civil War Cemetery. Ironically, only Northern dead were initially interred in the Sharpsburg cemetery, while some of the southern dead from the battle were buried in a mass grave in Hagerstown, Maryland, nine miles north of Sharpsburg.

Continuously, for 153 years, the town government or the American Legion, or in a few cases town civic leaders, have conducted a parade near the end of May of each year (Decorations Day, Memorial Day or whatever the day was referred to) to honor service members sacrifices in, initially, the Civil War, and later in all wars.

However, in 2020, by direction of the various governments and health organizations, the parade was officially canceled due to the COVID epidemic—yet a group of townspeople met with decorated autos at noon on Saturday the 23rd of May 2020, and paraded through town, horns blowing, to ensure the tradition remained alive. This past Saturday, the 154th edition of this memorial event took place as officially scheduled. Sharpsburg, with a population of less than 800 souls, knows the value of freedom and expresses that value each year with this wonderful and traditional Memorial Day event.

And just so you know why I, personally, always give the nod to Sharpsburg as the oldest celebration of Memorial Day. Over the 150-odd years, along with two Maryland governors, one U.S. President (Andrew Johnson attend the first parade), two Maryland lieutenant governors, numerous veterans, and perhaps most notably Mary Tyler Moore, in 2014, I was honored to be named the Grand Marshal of this Memorial Day parade—that honor ranks among the greatest bestowed on this undeserving veteran.

In a proclamation, General John A. Logan of the Grand Army of the Republic — an organization of former soldiers and sailors — dubbed May 30, 1868, Decoration Day, which was "designated for the purpose of strewing with flowers or otherwise decorating the graves of comrades who died in defense of their country during the late rebellion." On Decoration Day that year, General James Garfield gave a speech at Arlington National Cemetery. Afterward, five thousand observers adorned the graves of the more than twenty thousand Union and Confederate soldiers entombed at the cemetery.

At the outset, Memorial Day was so closely linked with the Union cause that many Southern states refused to celebrate it. They acquiesced only after World War I, when the holiday was expanded beyond honoring fallen Civil War soldiers to recognizing Americans who died fighting in all wars. It was also renamed Memorial Day. Some critics say that by making the holiday more inclusive, however, the original focus — on, as Frederick Douglass put it, the moral clash between "slavery and freedom, barbarism and civilization"—has been lost. Some Southern states still recognize Confederate Memorial Day as an official holiday, and many celebrate it on the June birthday of Jefferson Davis, the President of the Confederacy. But Texas, for one, observes Texas Hero's Day on Robert E. Lee's birthday, January 19.

The long-cherished Memorial Day tradition of wearing red poppies got its start in 1915. While reading *Ladies' Home Journal*, an overseas war secretary named Moina Michael came across the famous World War I poem *In Flanders Fields* by John McCrae, which begins, "In Flanders fields the poppies blow/Between the crosses, row on row." Moved, she vowed always to wear a silk poppy in honor of the American soldiers who gave up their lives for the freedom of others during WWI. She started selling red poppies to friends and co-workers, and campaigned for the red flowers to become an official memorial emblem.

Ms. Michael also wrote the following poem as a response to Army Lieutenant Colonel John McCrae's prose:

"Oh! You who sleep in Flanders fields,
Sleep sweet—to rise anew!
We caught the torch you threw
And holding high, we keep the Faith
With All who died
   We cherish, too, the poppy red
That grows on fields where valor led;
It seems to signal to the skies
That blood of heroes never dies,
But lends a luster to the red
Of the flower that blooms above the dead
In Flanders field
   And now the Torch and Poppy Red
We wear in honor of our dead
Fear not that ye have died for naught;
We'll teach the lesson that you wrought
In Flanders field"

The American Legion embraced the red poppy symbol in 1921, and the tradition has spread to more than fifty other countries, including England, France and Australia.

With the National Holiday Act of 1971, Congress moved Memorial Day from May 30 to the last Monday in May. But critics say guaranteeing that the holiday is part of a three-day weekend promotes relaxation instead of stressing the holiday's true meaning. In 1989, Senator Daniel Inouye of Hawaii (a WWII combat veteran and Medal of Honor winner) introduced a bill to move the holiday back to the fixed date of May 30. He reintroduced it in every Congress until his death in 2012—with no success. As for me, as you will hear later, I have always stood with Senator Inouye and reflect in memorial, each year, on the 30th of May.

While traditional Memorial Day rites have dwindled in many towns, they remain strong at Arlington National Cemetery. Since the 1950s, on the Thursday before Memorial Day, soldiers of the 3rd Infantry Division have placed American flags at each of the more than 260,000 graves there. During the weekend, they patrol around the clock to make sure each flag remains aloft. On the holiday itself, every year about five thousand people turn out to see the president or vice president give a speech and lay a wreath at the Tomb of the Unknown Soldier. And other Americans are encouraged to observe in a more solitary fashion. At 3 p.m. local time on the 31st of May each year, according to the 2000 National Moment of Remembrance Act, which was passed to emphasize the meaning of Memorial Day, all Americans should "voluntarily and informally observe in their own way a moment of remembrance and respect, pausing from whatever they are doing for a moment of silence or listening to *Taps*."

So, today, at 3 p.m., pause with other Americans for a moment and dwell on some of the following statements about Memorial Day, our Freedoms and Remembrance:

"Our debt to the heroic men and valiant women in the service of our country can never be repaid. They have earned our undying gratitude. America will never forget their sacrifices." —Harry S. Truman.

"A hero is someone who has given his or her life to something bigger than oneself." —Joseph Campbell.

"No arsenal, or no weapons in the arsenals of the world, is so formidable as the will and moral courage of free men and women." —Ronald Reagan

"My fellow Americans, ask not what your country can do for you, ask what you can do for your country." —John F. Kennedy.

"The highest obligation and privilege of citizenship is that of bearing arms for one's country." —George S. Patton, Jr.

"Heroes never die. They live on forever in the hearts and minds of those who would follow in their footsteps." —Emily Potter.

"The willingness of America's veterans to sacrifice for our country has earned them our lasting gratitude." —Jeff Miller.

I hope you heard in these glorious and meaningful words a respect and remembrance for more than those who died wearing the uniform of our nation. Campbell speak of "heroes;" Patton speaks honor; Kennedy speaks to "all Americans," not just those in uniform; and Reagan talks of "free men and women." As I have mentioned from this podium before, I ask each of you here today to remember not only soldiers, sailors, Marines, Air Force, Space Force and Coast Guard members, but to also remember doctors, nurses, first responders, security, police and fire personnel, and all those workers, living or dead who daily have spent and spend their lives to make us safe and secure and therefore assure us of life, liberty, happiness and above all else, freedom. So, what about freedom?

Some of you that know me know that my creed in life deals with the way you take on each new day. When you wake up each morning you have two choices: be happy or be sad. Most every day of the world I choose happy, with only one day a year reserved for sad. That day, this year and most every year, was yesterday—May 30, the traditional "Decorations Day" more commonly known today as Memorial Day.

Why, you may ask, are you sad on that one particular day? Well, I'm sad as I remember the sacrifices of those men and women who gave and/or dedicated their lives to allow us the freedoms we have today. You see, Memorial Day could, by my account, be called Remembrance Day, or maybe even better yet Freedoms Day. I'm sad because most of the men and women I remember have passed on after giving their lives for the freedoms you and I enjoy; and even more so, I'm sad that many of the freedoms we have enjoyed have been eroded over time, or in some cases lost—and that, my friends, is truly sad and mocks the sacrifice of those who gave their lives to allow us our freedom.

I spent a few moments earlier relating words from famous folks concerning Memorial Day, sacrifice and remembrance yet, in my own mind, I'm haunted each year by the words in a song written by a U.S. Army Reserve Captain, Kris Kristofferson, and sung best, to my taste, by Janis Joplin. The song is "Me and Bobby McGee." In its entirety, the song has little to do with memorials, or war, or sacrifice or corporate remembrance. But, once again yesterday, I drank a beer and sat and reflected on the one line from that song that speaks to my heart about the whole purpose of Memorial Day: That verse is, "Freedom's just another word for nothin' left to lose. Nothin', it ain't nothin' honey if it ain't free."

As Americans we have nothin' if we lose our freedoms, and we ain't nothin' if we ain't free. Thank God for those who have sacrificed for us and for our freedom. It is from those sacrifices that we remain free. And God Bless You and God Bless America. Thank you.

Very Respectfully, Art Callaham, Memorial Day 2021, Richmond, Texas.

Appendix

In Chapter 9 of the *Friends* section of this book, I listed (a short list, as it were) friends, family, acquaintances and folks who were close friends or, in some cases, just people I knew, who had a direct and positive bearing on my life. In that list I didn't list my mother and father (both passed away many years ago); my father- and mother-in-law (again, both passed away), my brother (whose own written words I used in one vignette), my brother- and sister-in-law (again, whose own written words I used in a couple of the chapters). I owe each of them an unrepayable debt of gratitude and love.

Although I'm sure I've still missed many, (and some are listed here and in Chapter 9 and other chapters), here are several others who knowingly or unknowingly have shaped my life:

Reverend "Spike" Callaham and Samantha Callaham Musso, best children—ever.

Chris Musso and Erica Moore Callaham, best spouses of my children—ever.

Ethan, Dominic, Hannah, Aaron, best grandchildren—ever.

Harry and Pat Reynolds, he's the chairman for the SOB's (Society of Bonders).

Bill and Linda Schelling, he's the provost for the SOB's.

Tim and Beth Rowland, without them this book would never have been published.

Carol Bruner Callaham, she takes care of Bert (my brother).

Bert Callaham, best brother - ever

Louise Standard, just like a sister to me.

Nichole Houser, took care of me in my best job ever, can't thank her enough.

Wayne Alter, great friend and mentor.

Ed Lough, great friend and mentor.

Jim Latimer, great friend and mentor.

CW5 Fred Shinbur, a veterans' veteran.

Chris McKinney, over 200 federal employees kept their job because of her efforts.

Carolyn Walker, another best friend.

Jack and Sandra Miller, he's a member of the SOB's.

Dan and Sue Duncan, brother and sister-in-law.

Brien and Chase Poffenberger, best friends.

Lou Scally, best radio and TV announcer—ever.

MAJ Warren McVey, top notch soldier.

LT "Wild Bill" McCall, shaped many OCS candidates—including me.

Greg Allen, high school friend.

"Butch" Woodrum, high school friend.

Allen Eckel, high school friend and Army buddy.

Cleo Mathews, high school teacher and friend.

Arthur Adkins, high school friend.

Steve and Linda Meadows, great friends.

Pam Vass, great friend.

Shelia Mould Wittington, great friend.

Peggy Lowe, great friend.

John and Pricilla Harsh, he's in the SOB's.

Dave and Julianne Harp, he's in the SOB's, best corned beef and cabbage ever.

Paul Muldowney, a great friend, mentor and best political mind I know.

Tom Kitchens, friend and great basketball coach.

Rhonda Saunders, high school friend.

The late Roy and Betty Galloway, great friends and family.

Denny, Chris and Lisa Galloway, great friends and family.

Jim and Pat Onem, great friends and family.

The late Wes and Tammy Lewis, great friends and family.

Ron Bowers, taught me a lot about politics.

Linda Kay Ward, high school friend.

Bonnie Chewning Young, great friend and organizer.

Janet Shinault Huff, great friend.

Dick and the late Roxanna Trump, neither related to "the Donald."

Jim Miller, friend, co-producer of radio and television, best ever.

Bob Bruchey, not a bad mayor.

James Kercheval, friend and best executive director of GHC.

Dr. P. Mark and Patty Divelbiss, he's in the SOB's, she taught me to play the piano.

Dr. Ed and Paula Lampton, they taught me a lot about being a Republican.

John Donoghue, worked hard for the Hagerstown community.

Don Munson, also worked hard for the Hagerstown community.

Benny Hogan, friend from High School.

Pat Farrell, friend from High School.

Larry Siehl, great friend.

The late Charles Swepton, friend from school and a good Marine.

Reverend Carl Meyers, if I make it to heaven, it will be because of him.

The late Tom and Ginny Lindsay, friend, mentor and number 1 golf buddy.

BG Jack Blair, good commander.

BG Bob Winn, good commander.

The late COL Jim Walsh, taught me when to pick your opportunities to not speak.

BG Fred Essig, good commander.

Bruce and Kathleen Poole, great friends and mentors

The late Mike Busch, Maryland Speaker of the House, great political mentor.

The late Mike Miller, Maryland President of the Senate, another mentor.

Carl and Judy Jamarik, great friends to this day.

The late Charlie and Madge Willis, great friend and mentor.

Tom Kuhn, great friend.

Dan Greenwald, good friend and a great bike rider.

Col. Clyde O. Brown, a soldier's soldier, should have become a Flag Officer.

The late Vernon Mugerditchan, taught me the ropes in civil service.

U.S. Senator Joe Manchin, although a Democrat, makes me proud to be from W.Va.

The Chairpersons: Bob Cirincione, (Jim Latimer, mentioned above), Bill Barton, Tom Newcomer, Jim Pierne, John League, Gaye McGovern—lead the best nonprofit ever.

The "Malaxis Cult": Tom and Linda Newell, Reg and Paula Holland, Berk and Jane Luhman, Ross and Pat Atkins, Jack and Mary Lesley, Betty Horton, Sharon McQuillan—they take care of me now.

The veterans: the late Jerry Ackerman, the late Bob Trotter, Ken Brockway, Jerry Brooks, Ric Stephan, Wes Ides, John Harrell, Ron Bordwell, Phil Gerber, Don Bagozzi, Judith Thomas, Andy Sugalski, Harry Shapiro, Charlie Graci, Bruce Gilman, Ray Wathen—they all know where it is.

Al and Lorie Cusik, they have brought me a clearer meaning of the "Word"

Mel and Liz Weaver, along with my wife, they certainly raised my kids

Stacey Chaney, great friend and the toughest fighter I know

Steve and Linda Meadows, high school friends

Kelly Honaker, knows about reunions
Ed Yates, best quarterback
Tammy Baker, along with Tim, best journalist I know
Jake Womer, great news editor
Lannie and Gary Base, Janice and Art Gonzales, Carla and John Kocian, Sally and Bill
Evans; Ruth Anne's posse and my friends.

Made in the USA
Columbia, SC
20 January 2024

181ef22b-2316-4ca6-9ce4-e52a97146591R01